YORKSHIRE
RAILWAYS

FEATURING IMAGES FROM
THE **YORKSHIRE POST**

Sheffield, South Yorkshire Railway Co. Ltd
The launch of the South Yorkshire Railway Founders' Club on 26 January 1993 is pictured here. The event took place at the base of the South Yorkshire Railway Co. Ltd, Meadowhall, Sheffield. At that time, the company had forty-five preserved locomotives, owned by both the society and individuals. The South Yorkshire Railway Co. Ltd left their Meadowhall site in 2002, finding a new home in Rowsley, Derbyshire, and have since become known as the Heritage Shunters Trust.

Leeds City Station
Geoff Bounds, pictured in January 1994, was in charge of a project that aimed to bring an end to the problems at the west end of Leeds City station.

YORKSHIRE RAILWAYS

FEATURING IMAGES FROM
THE **YORKSHIRE POST**

PETER TUFFREY

FONTHILL

Barnsley, Qualter Hall & Co. Ltd
Qualter Hall & Co. Ltd of Barnsley were responsible for producing the body shell for several new Eurotunnel Class 9 electric locomotives that had been ordered in 2000. Two are pictured at the company's premises during February 2003 and the final assembly would be completed by Brush Traction. The power of the locomotives was increased to 7MW over the 5.6MW of their predecessors, and they were to work the 'Le Shuttle' service, which transported road vehicles through the Eurotunnel.

FONTHILL MEDIA
www.fonthillmedia.com

Copyright © Peter Tuffrey 2013, 2016

First published 2013, reprinted 2016

ISBN 978-1-78155-316-9

A CIP catalogue record for this book is available from the British Library

Typeset in 10.5pt on 13pt Sabon LT Std
Typesetting by Fonthill Media
Printed in the UK

Contents

Acknowledgements

I am grateful for the assistance of the following people: Paul Bolton, Peter Charlton, David Clay, Paul License, Hugh Parkin, Jane Salt, Susan Tyler-Stringer.
    Special thanks are due to my son Tristram Tuffrey for his general help and advice.

Photographs
All photographs copyright *Yorkshire Post Newspapers*. View and buy the full range of pictures in this book by visiting yorkshirepost.co.uk or contact the photosales department on 0113 238 8360, giving a description of the picture.

Information
I have taken reasonable steps to verify the accuracy of the information in this book but it may contain errors or omissions. Any information that may be of assistance to rectify any problems will be gratefully received. Please contact me by email petertuffrey@rocketmail.com or in writing: Peter Tuffrey, 8 Wrightson Avenue, Warmsworth, Doncaster, South Yorkshire, DN4 9QL.

Leeds Station 91 001
The Class 91 electric locomotives were built to operate between London King's Cross and Edinburgh and all thirty-one members of the class were erected at Crewe Works between 1988 and 1991. The locomotives featured four GEC G426AZ traction motors that developed a maximum continual traction output of 6,090 hp. A top speed of 140 mph could be reached, but a limit was set at 125 mph. Between 2000 and 2002 the class was refurbished and renumbered 911xx. Electric locomotive no. 91 001 is pictured after arriving in Leeds on 20 September 1989.

Introduction

I suppose this book is a companion to an earlier one commissioned by Alan Sutton when he was Managing Director of Amberley Publishing. Now in the same position but fronting Fonthill Media, he was quite happy for me to produce another railway book delving into the archives at the *Yorkshire Post* newspaper. It was timely too, as the *Yorkshire Post* moved buildings at the end of 2012 and, as with any move, things turned up that were long forgotten. This was the case with a large box of 5x4 glass plate negatives that were located in a dark corner of the building. The photographs were obviously taken by a railway enthusiast (or even several) who, at one time, was on the *Yorkshire Post* photographic staff. With the odd exception, they cover a period between the late 1940s and early 1960s. They are marvellously crisp and capture a flavour of the time quite adequately.

Many of the photographs are featured in the Lineside section and the ones particularly poignant are the action shots of locomotives steaming at speed through a number of well-known locations in and around the Leeds and York areas. A perfect example of this is A3 60046 *Diamond Jubilee* on page 16, belching out smoke whilst passing Wortley South Junction with 'The White Rose' in October 1951. The picture on page 18 of 48673 in the Marsh Lane cutting captures a typical steam locomotive working in the area during the early 1950s. The pictures of locomotives working on the east coast main line are equally impressive. One example on page 32 features Peppercorn A1 Class Pacific no. 60145 *Saint Mungo* speeding through Otterington station in 1953 with 'The Flying Scotsman' service.

Several gems found amongst the glass plates include pictures of the Deltic prototype passing through Wakefield Westgate and Skipton station. Resplendent in bright blue livery, the locomotive must have starkly contrasted against the murky blacks and greens of steam engines trundling along on their last legs.

Two pictures included in the Lineside section are bound to cause a reaction if not concern from most railway enthusiasts. These show a Class 47 locomotive no. 47 134 passing through Rotherham in 1981 with a cargo of nuclear waste. A biologist and environmentalist commented: 'If only 10 per cent of a particular volatile material called Caesium 137 escaped in an area as heavily populated as Rotherham, 600 cancer deaths could be expected within a four-mile radius, and it would be 100 years before the people evacuated from the area could return.' Quite a sobering thought!

The earliest glass plate in the Lineside section is on page 9 and features LNER no. 10000 departing from Leeds New station. It is worthwhile comparing this engine with the electric locomotive seen on page 61 and appreciating how far locomotive development has progressed over the ensuing years.

The Marshalling Yards, Sheds and Works section abounds with pin-sharp locomotive portraits from glass plates. Of particular note is the one on page 68 showing Peppercorn A2 Class Pacific no. 60539 *Bronzino* near the mechanical coaler at Neville Hill shed. Another interesting batch of pictures shows the early days at Tinsley Marshalling Yard, Sheffield. None other than Lord Beeching opened the area, but sadly it is no longer extant.

Sadly the Yorkshire area has seen a number of bad rail crashes and one in particular is shown over pages 91 and 92. It depicts the aftermath of the collision on 31 July 1967 when the 12.00 p.m. King's Cross to Edinburgh express collided with a cement wagon at approximately 50 mph on the down fast line near Thirsk. Sadly seven people were killed and over forty injured. The ferocity of the collision is clearly evident by the damage sustained by the locomotive, DP2, which was withdrawn as a result of the collision. Several nasty incidents occurred on level crossings in the area and the hardy *Yorkshire Post* photographers and journalists were quick to record events and present public opinion on how further occurrences could be avoided. One of the most alarming stories in this section concerns the driver of a Class 47 locomotive who narrowly escaped serious injury in West Yorkshire when a reinforced concrete block was hurled at his windscreen. Spikes protruding from the block narrowly missed him otherwise he would have been seriously injured or even killed.

It has to be said that Yorkshire has some of the most impressive railway heritage centres in the country and it was difficult to decide which pictures to include and leave out. The North Yorkshire Moors Railway impressed one Dutchman so much that he helped finance the restoration of two locomotives. One has even been named after his mother Sybilla. The last section featuring stations, signal boxes, tunnels and bridges inevitably shows derelict stations which over the years have suffered terribly even though many contain impressive architectural features. Signal boxes, once an extremely common sight, have all but disappeared from the railway scene, but over the last few years they have generated great interest.

The final word must be for the *Yorkshire Post* photographers and journalists who over a number of decades recorded the railway scene in the county. This book hopes to provide more than a passing glimpse into their work.

CHAPTER 1
Lineside

Leeds New Station 10000
Dating from 7 July 1930, this image shows London & North Eastern Railway no. 10000 departing from Leeds New station with an unidentified passenger service. Leeds New station was the result of a connection between the North Eastern Railway's old station at Marsh Lane and the London & North Western Railway line at Leeds Junction. Both companies were involved in the construction of Leeds New station and initially it only had three platforms when opened to traffic on 1 April 1869. By the time of its combination with Leeds Wellington station on 2 May 1938, ten platforms were in use. The latter station had been opened on 1 October 1850 by the Midland Railway and replaced a temporary structure that had been operated by the company since 1 July 1846. Leeds Wellington station lay adjacent to the north of Leeds New station and when it joined, the number of platforms became sixteen. At this time the two became known as Leeds City station. No. 10000 had a disappointing performance record before its water tube boiler was removed and the locomotive received a conventional one during 1937, running in this form until its withdrawal in June 1959.

LMS 3P no. 195

Pictured just after Nationalisation in March 1948, with its LMS identity still readily apparent, is Stanier 3P Class 2-6-2T locomotive no. 195, later BR no. 40195. Construction was carried out at Crewe Works during December 1937 and the engine's career lasted until November 1961 when it was withdrawn. At the time of this picture the locomotive was allocated to Farnley Junction shed, but by 1950 it had reached Southport. No. 40195 was transferred to Kirkby-in-Ashfield for its last allocation in September 1961. The 3P Class design was based on the Fowler 3P 2-6-2T engines, but the former featured Stanier's taper boiler amongst some other changes.

LMS 2730

Designed by George Hughes, this 2-6-0 locomotive entered service in November 1926 as LMS no. 13030. On 19 February 1935, it was renumbered 2730, then 42730 in 1948. The photograph dates from 24 March 1948, when the engine was allocated to 25G – Farnley Junction. Withdrawal came on 26 June 1965 from Stockport Edgeley shed.

Leeds Central Station No. 3
Departing from Leeds Central station on 18 March 1948, possibly with a service bound for the capital, is LNER Gresley A4 Pacific no. 3 *Andrew K. McCosh*. The locomotive entered traffic from Doncaster Works in August 1937 as LNER no. 4494 *Osprey*, but was renamed *Andrew K. McCosh* in October 1942 after the LNER's Chairman of the Locomotive Committee. No. 3 had been carried since September 1946 as part of that year's renumbering scheme, and the locomotive's BR number – 60003 – was acquired in March 1949. Withdrawal occurred on 29 December 1962 with four other A4s, which were the first withdrawals of the A4 class by BR.

Leeds City Station 44754

A month after entering traffic with Caprotti valve gear at the start of April 1948 is Class 5 no. 44754, setting off from Leeds City station on a run to Edinburgh. The locomotive was allocated to Leeds Holbeck shed from new until September 1961 when a reallocation to Stockport occurred. At the end of 1961 Speke Junction became both no. 44754's new and final home, residing there until leaving service in April 1964. The engine has a scroll and serif smokebox number plate and 10-in.-high cab side numerals.

Danby Wiske 976

Built by Darlington Works in October 1943, Class V2 2-6-2 locomotive No. 976 is pictured displaying its second Grouping number. Initially no. 3688 and later no. 60976, the engine is hurtling through Danby Wiske during May 1948 when it was allocated to York shed. The locomotive was withdrawn from St Margaret's in September 1966 and subsequently scrapped at Cambells, Airdrie.

Leeds City Station 45079
When constructed as Leeds New, the station was situated on an area of land that was traversed by the River Aire and the Leeds & Liverpool Canal. As a result it had to be raised above them using a series of brick vaults and bridges. The station was subsequently expanded in the late-1870s and a new train shed was required. This was designed by Thomas Prosser and T. E. Harrison and featured a Mansard roof that was supported by cast-iron columns and spandrel panels. This is illustrated in this picture along with the 1890s western expansion of the train shed by William Bell. This had a transverse pitched roof that was supported by lattice girders and columns. Stood under these two portions of the station with its train is Stanier Class 5 no. 45079, which was constructed by the Vulcan Foundry in March 1935 and withdrawn thirty-two years later in March 1967. The photograph dates from 8 October 1951.

Harrogate 46485
Approaching Harrogate station from the north on 29 November 1951 is Ivatt Class 2 2-6-0 no. 46485. The locomotive was constructed at Darlington Works in November 1951 and might be on its way to begin work at Newton Heath shed. Thirty-eight members of the class were built at Darlington between 1951 and 1952, with the remainder being the product of Crewe (sixty-five) and Swindon (twenty-five). Allocation to Newton Heath lasted until March 1953 when the locomotive's longest allocation to Agecroft shed began; the engine was based there eight years and three months. A number of moves occurred in no. 46485's final years, including a return to Newton Heath before withdrawal claimed the locomotive in June 1967. Seen to the right of the engine is Harrogate North signal box, which is still in use, but is now named just Harrogate signal box.

Kildwick & Crosshills Station 41069
This image was captured at the site of the old Kildwick & Crosshills station, which was opened in early 1848 by the Leeds and Bradford Railway on their extension line to Colne. The station's name was originally just Kildwick and before the mid-1880s, when the station's title became fixed, the variants Kildwick for Cross Hills and Kildwick & Cross Hills were used. On 7 April 1889 a new station was built slightly to the west of the site seen here and it was in use until 22 March 1965. The building seen to the left of the locomotive was part of the old station's goods yard and out of view to the left was the station building; both of these are still in existence as commercial premises and a private residence respectively.

Kirkstall 45265
 Saltley-based Class 5 no. 45265 passes Kirkstall power station northbound on the slow line between Leeds and Shipley with an unidentified passenger service during the early 1950s. At the beginning of the twentieth century the line was increased to four tracks to separate the local traffic from the longer distance workings; however, the line reverted back to two tracks in the late 1960s. Kirkstall power station became operational in 1931 and generated electricity until its closure in 1976. By 1985 the site was cleared and the land was converted into a golf course and nature reserve.

Spurn Point Light Railway

Just before the First World War, the War Department recognised the danger posed to the east coast ports and set about erecting some fortifications to protect them. Spurn Point was chosen as the site for a gun battery of 4-in. guns and, to transport men and materials to the site, a railway was constructed. The line was 3¾ miles long between Kilnsea and Spurn Point, with 0-4-0ST locomotives being used on the track. Two bogies were also utilised for transporting people and they were powered through sails. In the early 1950s the line was deemed unnecessary and the last trip was made by this coach in 1951.

Leeds 60046

Passing Wortley South Junction during October 1951, no. 60046 *Diamond Jubilee* is with 'The White Rose'. As LNER no. 2545, the engine received a streamlined non-corridor tender (no. 5644) during June 1937. This was because the corridor tenders in the possession of A1 and A3 locomotives were given to new A4 Class engines, but no. 2545 had a coal rail tender at this time so the reason for the switch is obscure. The tender remained with the locomotive for the rest of its career and is seen here painted in BR blue, which had been acquired in August 1949.

Opposite below: **Leeds 60855**

Gresley V2 Class 2-6-2 no. 60855 passes Copley Hill shed at Wortley South Junction with an unidentified passenger service on 17 October 1951. The engine was one of twenty-eight V2 Class locomotives built at Darlington in 1939. No. 60855 began work in April from King's Cross shed as LNER no. 4826. At the time of this picture the locomotive was a Peterborough New England engine and had been there since transferring from King's Cross in July 1940. No. 60855 had a number of moves in the London area before York became the engine's final shed in November 1958. The locomotive left service in April 1964. Seen in the background outside Copley Hill shed is V2 no. 60913, which was a few days into its allocation having arrived on 14 October 1951; it left for Tweedmouth in September 1958.

Leeds 60046

Another view of LNER Gresley A1 Pacific no. 60046 *Diamond Jubilee* which was built at Doncaster Works in August 1924. The locomotive was the third A1 Class engine to be constructed there during the year and a further seventeen had entered traffic when the production run stopped in July 1925; these locomotives took LNER nos 2543-2562. Photographed during October 1951, no. 60046 *Diamond Jubilee* (A3 since August 1941) is heading 'The White Rose' passenger service, which ran between Bradford Exchange, Leeds City and London King's Cross. The engine was a Doncaster resident at this time and had a number of spells at Eastern Region sheds before its career came to an end in June 1963; it was then scrapped at Doncaster.

Leeds, Marsh Lane 48673
Heading towards the Neville Hill end of Marsh Lane cutting with a tank train on 20 November 1951 is LMS Stanier 8F 2-8-0 no. 48673. The locomotive was constructed at Ashford Works during March 1944 as part of an order from the Railway Executive Committee. Two hundred and forty-five 8Fs were built for the REC between 1943 and 1945 at a number of different Works. The Southern Railway's Works at Brighton, Eastleigh and Ashford produced 105 REC engines, yet, unlike the GWR and LNER, the SR did not operate any of these engines and they were transferred to the LMS. No. 48673 was allocated to Birkenhead at the time of this picture, but after a number of moves would leave service from Stockport Edgeley shed in November 1967.

Harrogate 62736

The Gresley D49 Class of 4-4-0 locomotives was built to replace life-expired NER and North British Railway passenger engines; seventy-six were constructed between 1927 and 1935. Three class parts existed as Gresley experimented with a number of valve gear arrangements. No. 62736, as LNER no. 201, was erected at Darlington Works in April 1932 with rotary cam operated Lentz poppet valves placing it in class part two. Forty-two locomotives formed this class part and all were named after hunts, with the two engines initially constructed with the valve gear changing their name from the 'shire' originally carried. No. 62736 carried the name *The Bramham Moor* after the hunt which took place in the Wetherby and Harwood area of West Yorkshire. The locomotive is pictured at Harrogate on 29 November 1951.

Doncaster Station 60064

No. 60064 *Tagalie* was based in Scotland until 1950 and had been allocated to Edinburgh Haymarket, Aberdeen, Glasgow Eastfield, Edinburgh St Margaret's and Dundee. The locomotive was built by the North British Locomotive Company at their Hyde Park Works in July 1924. Twenty were constructed by the company in total (LNER nos 2563-2582) and they entered traffic during 1924. No. 60064 was originally numbered 2563 and named *William Whitelaw* when it was completed. Renaming occurred in August 1941 so the original name could be transferred to A4 no. 4462 *Great Snipe*. No. 60064 was allocated to Doncaster from Haymarket in July 1950 and it is seen here at Doncaster station on 27 March 1952. *Tagalie* was removed from service in September 1961.

Doncaster Station 60146

In January 1947 an engine order was placed at Darlington for twenty-three Pacific locomotives, which would eventually form part of the Peppercorn A1 Class. No. 60146 *Peregrine* was completed at the Works in April 1949 towards the end of the batch. A distinguishing feature of the Darlington engines concerns the tender, which was fabricated using countersunk rivets leaving the sides flush, whereas the Doncaster tenders had snap head rivets that protruded from the side sheets. *Peregrine* also has electric lighting fitted, with the Stone's generator visible in front of the deflector plate. No. 60146 is pictured in March 1952 leaving Doncaster station with a service bound for King's Cross. *Peregrine*'s withdrawal occurred in October 1965.

Arksey 60501
Pictured at Arksey, just north of Doncaster, on 20 June 1952 with a Colchester–York express passenger service is no. 60501 *Cock o' the North*. The locomotive is seen in its rebuilt form as a Pacific, but it had started its career with a 'Mikado' or 2-8-2 wheel arrangement. *Cock o' the North*, the first member of Gresley's P2 Class to be erected at Doncaster in May 1934, was followed by further 5 Class members by September 1936. After Gresley's death in 1941, Edward Thompson took over the position of Chief Mechanical Engineer and decided the P2 Class members were ripe for rebuilding. As LNER no. 2001, the engine was the third to undergo the transformation, re-entering traffic in September 1944.

Doncaster 60112
'The Northumbrian' passenger service operated from 1949 to 1963 and ran between King's Cross and Newcastle. Approaching Doncaster on 26 June 1952 with the service is no. 60112 *St Simon*, which was built at the town's Works in September 1923 and was later re-built to A3 at the same location in August 1946. No. 60112 was based at Grantham when the picture was taken and had a number of spells working from the shed. The locomotive was withdrawn from Peterborough New England shed in December 1964.

Arksey 63956

This locomotive was the second of a batch of eight Gresley O2 Class 2-8-0s to be erected between November 1933 and March 1934; this engine, as LNER no. 2431, entered traffic from Doncaster in December. The locomotive was of an upgraded design to the O2s that had been built in the early 1920s. Some of the new features were left-hand drive, steam brakes, new valve gear arrangement, carriage warming apparatus on the tender and side window cab. This engine also received a second-hand Group Standard tender from a J38 Class 0-6-0 when new and the type is still attached to no. 63956, which is seen at Arksey with a coal train on 26 June 1952. Withdrawal from Grantham took place during September 1963.

Arksey 60876

A Doncaster-built V2, no. 60876, is pictured at Arksey with a fast freight on 26 June 1952. No. 60876 had been constructed in May 1940 and for the first six years of its career carried LNER no. 4847. The engine became no. 876 in the 1946 renumbering and BR applied their number during October 1948. From new, the allocation was to Peterborough New England, but after a number of moves during the mid-1950s the locomotive joined the V2 contingent at York in November 1958 and was later relieved of its duties at the shed in October 1965.

Stourton 43014

Ivatt Class 4 2-6-0 no. 43014 was manufactured at Horwich Works in April 1948. The engine poses for the camera at Stourton shed in July 1952 and features a double chimney, which was fitted to the first fifty that were built at Horwich. However, they were subsequently removed and no. 43014 was altered in August 1954. The locomotive had arrived relatively recently at Stourton, being four months into its allocation, which lasted a further seven years and four months. The engine was then sent to York and Manningham before its career ended in April 1966.

Stourton 11001

Located to the north of Woodlesford station, Stourton shed was built for the Midland Railway in 1893 and the building was a square roundhouse. Shunting some coal wagons in the shed's yard is diesel-mechanical locomotive no. 11001. The design was produced by O. V. S. Bulleid and it was built at Ashford Works in 1949. The locomotive was initially based at Norwood Junction before moving on loan to Feltham and then Stourton in July 1952; the locomotive is seen here not long after arriving. Stourton shed closed at the start of 1967 and the site is now a Freightliner depot.

Leeds Copley Hill 60865

Approaching Leeds Central station through the Copley Hill area with an unidentified passenger service is V2 Class locomotive no. 60865. The engine was a product of Darlington Works, which completed construction in June 1939. A number of tender varieties existed within the V2 Class and initially the locomotive would have been paired with the straight-sided type with a high front, but this has since been exchanged with one with stepped out sides. This would have originally been with a V2 built in 1938, nos 4804-4814, which in turn had come second hand from either a J39 or D49 Class locomotive. No. 60865 had been a Copley Hill resident for ten months when this picture was taken and it would move on to Tweedmouth in September 1958. The locomotive left service from Gateshead in June 1965.

Leeds Copley Hill Shed 60029

Arriving at Copley Hill shed on 1 August 1952 is King's Cross resident *Woodcock*. The locomotive was erected at Doncaster Works in July 1937 as LNER no. 4493 and it entered traffic with the LNER's standard green livery and lining applied. During the following July the engine was repainted in Garter blue with red lining as part of the standardisation of the A4 class livery, which was implemented because many variations existed at the time. After Nationalisation no. 60029 was one of four class members to take part in trials with different liveries and during July 1948 it was painted purple, with lining in grey, cream and red. At the time of this picture the locomotive had BR blue applied and was only two months away from receiving the Brunswick green livery. *Woodcock* left service in October 1963 after four months' allocation to Peterborough New England shed.

Leeds Copley Hill 60055
This A1 Class locomotive was built at Doncaster in December 1924 and given LNER no. 2554. Doncaster was the engine's first shed and it was there until April 1927 when transferred south to Grantham. Between April and June 1942 the locomotive was rebuilt to A3 specifications and at this time also received a different GNR tender with coal rails (no. 5211). This picture was taken on 1 August 1952 and shows BR no. 60055 *Woolwinder* at Copley Hill with the 15.20 service to King's Cross. The locomotive had a brief allocation to Copley Hill shed between October 1943 and December 1944, and then moved to see out the decade at King's Cross shed. Doncaster was again the locomotive's home from June 1950 to June 1956. Withdrawal occurred in September 1961.

Leeds City Station 43098
Ivatt Class 4 no. 43098 is with an unidentified passenger service at Leeds City station in mid-December 1952. Constructed at Darlington in February 1951, the engine was one of thirty-seven to be built there. Horwich Works produced seventy-five, while Doncaster contributed a further fifty to the class total. Selby was no. 43098's residence at the time of this picture and the locomotive would remain there until September 1959 when it moved to Goole. In October 1965 a re-allocation to Normanton occurred and the engine was relieved of its duties while there in May 1967.

Sessay 60975
Another V2 disturbs the quietness of Sessay station, this time with an express from Liverpool to Newcastle. No. 60975 was built at Darlington Works in mid-September 1943 – a month after no. 60974. Both were constructed as part of the final order for V2 Class locomotives, which was placed at Darlington in August 1941 and consisted of twenty-one engines. The order had originally been placed at Doncaster in April but it was switched with an order at Darlington for O2 Class locomotives. No. 60975 was also a long-term York resident and was there throughout its career, which ended in May 1964. Disposal was later carried out by Swindon Works.

Opposite above: **Stourton 45675**
Photographed at Stourton, passing a train with cattle wagons on the left, is LMS Stanier 'Jubilee' Class 4-6-0 no. 45675 *Hardy*. The locomotive is heading a passenger service that had originated in London and was destined for Newcastle. No. 45675 was erected at Crewe Works during December 1935, but it was not named *Hardy* until March 1937 while allocated to Carlisle Upperby shed. In November 1941 the locomotive began work from Crewe North shed and it was not until October 1948 that the engine reported for duty at Leeds Holbeck, initially on loan. The move was made permanent in November and *Hardy* was withdrawn from the shed in June 1967.

Opposite below: **Sessay 60974**
Sessay station was opened by the Great North of England Railway on 31 March 1841. It was approximately 18 miles from York and 12 miles from Northallerton. Speeding through the station with a Colchester to Newcastle passenger service is V2 no. 60974. The locomotive spent its twenty-year-long career allocated to York and was removed from service in December 1963, eventually being scrapped at Darlington. The station was closed on 15 September 1958.

Killingbeck 61239

This Thompson B1 is heading a York passenger train through Killingbeck cutting during May 1953; Killingbeck signal box is discernable behind the first and second carriages. The B1 Class locomotives featured 6 ft 2 in. diameter driving wheels, two cylinders measuring 20 in. diameter by 26 in. stroke, 10 in. piston valves and Walschaerts valve gear. No. 61239 was erected by the NBLC in October 1947 and withdrawn in August 1962 after entering Gorton Works for repair.

Killingbeck 61259

This view was captured from a footbridge over the line at Killingbeck, which is visible in the background of the picture of no. 61239. The line was opened by the Leeds & Selby Railway on 22 September 1834 mainly to serve goods traffic for the Knottingley & Goole Canal, which had been opened in 1826 to provide a connection with the port at Hull. The route left Leeds from Marsh Lane station and intermediate stations were at Garforth, Micklefield, Milford and Hambleton, with all except the latter still in use. No. 61259 is photographed in charge of a Leeds–Northallerton express during May 1953.

Horton-in-Ribblesdale 44757

Ex-London Midland & Scottish Railway Stanier Class 5 or 'Black Five' 4-6-0 no. 44757 hauls a heavy freight train (thirty-eight wagons) on the Settle to Carlisle line on 8 July 1953. One of the 'Yorkshire Three Peaks', Pen-y-ghent, forms the backdrop for the locomotive. No. 44757 has passed Horton-in-Ribblesdale station and is on the 'long drag' from Settle, which sees gradients of 1 in 100 and 1 in 200 take the line up to over 1,000 ft above sea level. The engine was the last of twenty Class 5s to be constructed between June and December 1948 with Caprotti valve gear. Other new features carried by these locomotives included a double chimney, electric lighting and Timken roller bearings. No. 44757 was allocated to Leeds Holbeck shed from new until moving to Lower Darwen shed, Blackburn, in March 1963. It was withdrawn from Southport in November 1965.

Otterington 60145

Peppercorn A1 Class Pacific no. 60145 *Saint Mungo* speeds through Otterington station with 'The Flying Scotsman' service in 1953. The locomotive was one of the last two class members to be withdrawn in March 1966; however, the engine was given a reprieve and returned to service in April. Only two months passed before its career finally came to an end. Otterington station was opened by the Great North of England Railway on 31 March 1841 and was later rebuilt by the LNER in 1932 to accommodate two new tracks (seen to the right and left of the locomotive). Closure came on 15 September 1958.

Kildwick & Crosshills Station 44987

No. 44987 was built at Horwich Works in November 1946 and was amongst the first of the Class 5s to be fitted with axlebox dust shields and a revised position for the oil required for axlebox lubrication. In April 1953 authorisation was given to change the locomotives not fitted with the arrangement when new, but the task was discontinued and incomplete at the end of 1958. No. 44987 is seen near Kildwick & Crosshills station, a short distance to the east of the crossing where the picture of no. 41069 was taken, with a service from Edinburgh bound for St Pancras station. Newton Heath was the engine's residence at Nationalisation until February 1953 when it moved to Wakefield. Only a month was spent at the latter location and the locomotive moved to Agecroft in March 1953. No. 44987 was withdrawn from Carnforth in October 1966.

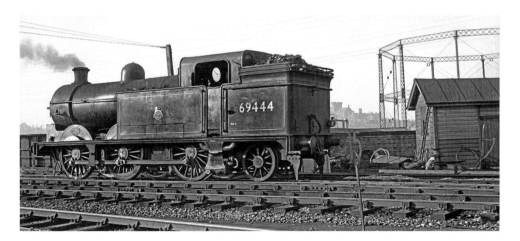

Leeds, Holbeck Low Level Station 69444

On a shunting duty at Leeds Holbeck Low Level station in the mid-1950s is Great Northern Railway Class N1 0-6-2T, designed by H. A. Ivatt. The locomotive was built at Doncaster Works in March 1910 and entered service as GNR no. 1564. It was originally fitted with condensing equipment to allow working in the London area, as were forty-nine of the fifty-four class members. Yet in May 1921 no. 69444 had the apparatus removed when transferred to the West Riding of Yorkshire from London; other locomotives that made the journey received the same attention. The engine was allocated to Copley Hill during the early 1950s, but was withdrawn in October 1956.

Kildwick & Crosshills Station 45040

Another picture taken near Kildwick & Crosshills station at the level crossing on the A6068 captures Stanier Class 5 no. 45040. The locomotive was erected by the Vulcan Foundry, Newton-le-Willows, in October 1934 and it carried boiler no. 8657 when new, which had a vertical firebox throatplate and fourteen superheater elements. During November 1936 the engine was modified at Crewe Works to accept the sloping firebox throatplate boiler and this necessitated moving a cross stay in addition to revising the front of the dragbox. The locomotive was a Saltley resident at the time of the photograph and the allocation began in September 1950, lasting until November 1956. Withdrawal from Crewe South occurred in July 1967.

Kirkstall 44854
Passing Kirkstall power station in the first half of the 1950s is Class 5 no. 44854. Crewe Works was the place of manufacture and the engine was completed in December 1944 with a Mark Two tender, no. 10479, which had modified spring links; the Mark Two tender type was carried throughout the locomotive's time in service. Between Nationalisation and September 1967 – no. 44854's date of withdrawal – the engine was housed at Leeds Holbeck shed.

Arthington 40148

With the Leeds–Ilkley service at Arthington is Stanier 3P no. 40148. The engine was constructed in August 1937 at Derby Works with an improved boiler from those originally fitted to nos 40071-40144. The 6A boilers featured a separate dome and top feed arrangement as well as an increased heating surface in the firebox, tubes and superheater. Six of the class were subsequently fitted with a 6B boiler, which further enhanced the heating surface figures. No. 40148 resided at Leeds Holbeck in the first half of the 1950s before moving to Sheffield Millhouses shed and then Royston. The engine was condemned in August 1962.

Skipton Deltic

Between August and September 1956 the prototype diesel-electric locomotive *Deltic* underwent trials on the Settle to Carlisle line and it is seen during this period at Skipton station. The trials were organised by the British Transport Commission and English Electric (the builder of the locomotive) with a train that consisted of twenty coaches, weighing 642 tons tare.

Deltic

Deltic is photographed with a test train (dynamometer car and two testing units) at an unidentified location, perhaps somewhere on the Settle–Carlisle line.

Wakefield Westgate Station Deltic

Deltic was completed in October 1955 at English Electric's Preston Works. The locomotive then went for static testing at Napiers' Nethertown Works and was subsequently allocated to the London Midland Region at Speke Junction. From the shed the locomotive worked a variety of services to test its capabilities. In January 1959 *Deltic* transferred to the Eastern Region to be used on east coast main line services and was found capable enough for BR to order twenty-two production locomotives to a similar design. These were built at Vulcan Foundry between January 1961 and May 1962 and were designated Class 55 by British Railways. After an engine failure, *Deltic* was withdrawn in March 1961 and was then restored by English Electric. The company donated the locomotive to the Science Museum in April 1963, but in 1993 it was given to the National Railway Museum and now forms part of their collection.

Hull Paragon Station E50363
Class 106 DMU no. E50363 was constructed by Cravens Railway Carriage and Wagon Company Ltd, Sheffield, in December 1956 and was based at Hull Springhead shed. E50363 was paired with E56118 and they were DMBS-DTCL vehicles. Fourteen of the sets were constructed and all were based in Hull to work in the local area, but they were later transferred to the London Region. The DMU is pictured at Hull Paragon station during mid-1957, ready to depart with a local service.

Leeds Central 61114
Doncaster resident, LNER Thompson B1 Class 4-6-0 no. 61114 is seen at Leeds Central station in March 1957 with a service bound for Northallerton. The locomotive was constructed by the North British Locomotive Company in January 1947 and was initially allocated to King's Cross shed. No. 61114 had two spells at Hitchin in 1948 before being transferred to Gorton in January 1949. A return to the London area occurred in October 1952 when Stratford was the locomotive's base and then in February 1954 Doncaster residency began. The final move to Immingham happened in December 1959 and two years were spent there before withdrawal in September 1962.

Arthington 61035

This B1 was built in October 1947 at Darlington Works, which produced forty members of the class between 1942 and 1947 and a further twenty in 1949/1950. Thirty-nine of the first forty built at Darlington carried the name of a type of antelope, while the anomaly was named after a LNER director. No. 61035 was named *Pronghorn*, after an antelope found in North America, when it entered service to York. No. 61035 was allocated to Neville Hill in April 1948 until January 1961, when it moved to Blaydon. Dating from March 1957 the picture shows *Pronghorn* with a Leeds to Northallerton service at Arthington. The locomotive was condemned while at York in December 1966.

Opposite above: **Wharfedale 60060**

No. 60060 *The Tetrarch* heads an unidentified train of BR standard carriages through Wharfedale in April 1957. The engine was erected in April 1925 and later took its name from the winner of the Champagne Stakes at Doncaster in 1913. Only four members of the A1 Class entered traffic with a name and between April 1925 and February 1926 the remaining nameless locomotives acquired one, which in the majority of cases came from a racehorse that had triumphed in a classic race. The locomotive was working from Gateshead shed at the time of the photograph and had been working from the North East since 1939. *The Tetrarch* was condemned in September 1963 and later scrapped at Darlington.

Opposite below: **Bramhope Tunnel 61415**

Originally belonging to NER Class S3 designed by Vincent Raven, this locomotive was subsequently re-classified B16 by the LNER after Grouping. As NER no. 915 the engine left Darlington Works in September 1920 to begin work from York North shed, which had a large contingent of the class based there throughout their time in service. After Nationalisation the number allocated to Neville Hill grew, with the shed being supplemented by a number from York; amongst these was no. 61415, which arrived in August 1949. The locomotive is pictured in July 1957 before entering Bramhope tunnel while assisting no. 60081 *Shotover*, which is in charge of a Liverpool express.

Arthington 60085
Production of new A3 Class Pacific locomotives commenced in August 1928 and ten had been produced by mid-1929. A further eight were completed during 1930 with this engine, LNER no. 2596 *Manna*, being part of the batch. Amongst the new features of these locomotives was the provision of a new type of non-corridor tenders. These had the same water and coal capacity as the GNR type, but the side sheets extended upwards to replace the coal rails and they were built to conform with the new left-hand driving position. *Manna* was initially paired with tender no. 5477 when it entered traffic in February 1930, but this was later replaced with tender no. 5483 of the same type in March 1937. A streamlined non-corridor tender was coupled for a month between February and March 1946 before tender no. 5483 was re-attached. No. 60085 ended its career in October 1964 with a GNR tender, which had been with the engine since April 1962.

Arthington 60153
The last batch of ten Peppercorn A1 Class locomotives was ordered from Doncaster Works in August 1948. No. 60153 was the first of this batch to enter traffic at the end of August 1949, while the last, no. 60162 *Saint Johnstoun*, was completed during December. No. 60153 did not receive its name – *Flamboyant* – until August 1950 and just one member of the class carried a name from new. No. 60153 was only allocated to York shed during its career and it is seen here at Arthington with a Newcastle–Leeds service in March 1958. *Flamboyant* ceased to be in service from 2 November 1962 and it was later cut up at Doncaster Works.

Arthington 60501
Thompson A2/2 no. 60501 *Cock o' the North* passes through Arthington with an unidentified passenger service. After being rebuilt the locomotive returned to work in Scotland until the whole class were relocated to England between 1949/1950. No. 60501 found a home at York, but it later had a spell at Neville Hill from November to December 1950 before returning to York. Fast goods services such as the Newcastle to King's Cross as well as returns could be worked by the locomotive in addition to passenger services to and from the capital. A difference seen in this picture of *Cock o' the North* from the one taken at Arksey is the lowering of the smokebox number plate. This occurred in September 1956 so the top lamp iron could be re-situated in its original lower position. No. 60501 was condemned in February 1960.

Arthington 60081

Passing through Arthington with 'The Queen of Scots' passenger service is no. 60081 *Shotover*. The locomotive had an early conversion to A3 which took place in February 1928. During a general repair between April and July 1929 at Darlington, *Shotover* was fitted with an A.C.F.I. feedwater heater. The locomotive carried the A.C.F.I. equipment until February 1939, with any improvements in the engine's performance offset by high maintenance and difficulty in operating it effectively. No. 60081 was allocated to Neville Hill shed from February 1949 until its withdrawal in October 1962.

Opposite above: **Arthington 40140**

Arthington station is the next stop for this local train that had begun its journey at Ilkley in March 1958. Otley and Pool-in-Wharfedale had been visited prior to this stop and the locomotive would then head to Leeds. Stanier 3P 2-6-2T no. 40140 was erected at Derby Works in October 1935 with a domeless boiler. Leeds Holbeck became the locomotive's final shed in July 1955. No. 40140 was removed from service in November 1961. Seen above the cab is a NER-type water tower.

Opposite below: **Holbeck 60078**

Gateshead resident no. 60078 *Night Hawk* passes through Holbeck, Leeds, during April 1958 with a passenger service bound for Liverpool. The locomotive had been built by the NBLC in October 1924 and was based at Gateshead from new until a move took it to York in January 1937. Between December 1943 and January 1944, *Night Hawk* was rebuilt to A3 specifications and it was given a diagram 94A boiler, no. 8779, which had come from A3 no. 2503 *Firdaussi*. The 94A boilers were very similar to the diagram 94HP boilers, but the former featured a perforated steam collector and 'banjo' shaped dome. Many locomotives used both types during their time in service, however, a number were only fitted with the 94A boiler, with no. 60076 being amongst them. *Night Hawk* was withdrawn from Heaton in October 1962 and cut up at Doncaster in mid-1963.

Arthington 60071

No. 60071 *Tranquil* was erected by the NBLC in September 1924 and when entering service it was dual-fitted with vacuum ejector and Westinghouse braking equipment. LNER nos. 2568-2582 of the NBLC-built batch were also fitted in this manner as they were to work in the north-eastern area, which employed the latter apparatus. During 1928 the LNER made the decision to use steam and vacuum brakes as standard on all locomotives and coaching stock. As a result the A1 Class Pacifics with Westinghouse brakes had them removed between 1933-35; *Tranquil* had the type taken off in October 1933. No. 60071 is seen approaching Arthington after leaving Bramhope tunnel in June 1958.

Arthington 61478
Construction of the NER S3 Class of 4-6-0 locomotives began in December 1919 and five batches were erected at Darlington. When the last was completed in January 1924 the total stood at seventy locomotives. No. 61478 was the last of the first batch to be completed and was ready for service in April 1920. These engines were originally to be numbered 61400-61409 after Nationalisation, but because of the final Thompson B1 Class taking up these numbers the B16s were placed at the end of the class numbering (61469-61478). At the head of this Wetherby races special, no. 61478 looks resplendent on the Otley loop line at Arthington in the summer of 1958.

Opposite below: **Ilkley 60074**
Gresley A1 Pacific *Harvester*, originally LNER no. 2573, was constructed in October 1924 by the NBLC, although its time as part of the A1 Class was quite short. In March 1927 five A3 boilers (diagram 94HP) were constructed and during July the first was fitted to LNER no. 4480 *Enterprise*. No. 2573 was the penultimate locomotive to receive a new A3 boiler in April 1928, with the last going to LNER no. 2578 *Bayardo* in May. These two locomotives, as well as LNER no. 2580 *Shotover*, have the distinction of being the only A1 Class engines to be rebuilt to A3 at Darlington Works, as the other A1 locomotives were rebuilt at Doncaster between November 1939 and December 1948. This photograph was taken in the Ilkley area during June 1958 and sees *Harvester* with an unidentified special service.

Arthington 61321

No. 61321 was built as part of the second NBLC order and entered traffic from the company's Queens Park Works in May 1948 to Borough Gardens. In 1958 moves to Wakefield and Darlington were completed; the locomotive was working from the latter when this picture was taken at Arthington in 1958 with a Harrogate to King's Cross service. No. 61321 was removed from service in August 1964 while based at Ardsley shed.

No. 44675

Stanier Class 5 4-6-0 no. 44675 is assisting an unidentified LMS 'Jubilee' 4-6-0 with a Leeds to Carlisle passenger service in July 1958. No. 44675 was a product of Horwich Works and had entered service in March 1950. The locomotive was part of the roller-bearing experiments and had SKF bearings fitted to the driving axle only.

Bramhope 60076

Gresley A1 Pacific no. 2575 *Galopin* was erected at the NBLC's Hyde Park Works during October 1924 and entered traffic to Gateshead. The locomotive was rebuilt to A3 in June 1941 and it was the first such undertaking of the year, with five other A1s following in the subsequent six months. In September 1948 *Galopin* received BR no. 60076 and at the end of the year the locomotive's first shed transfer occurred when it moved to Darlington. The shed used no. 60076 on pilot work, which decreased the frequency of its visits to Works and as a result the engine was one of two not to receive BR blue livery. Darlington resident no. 60070 *Gladiateur* was the other locomotive and it was also used as a pilot. *Galopin* is seen hard at work approaching Bramhope tunnel with the Liverpool to Newcastle express in the summer of 1958.

Arthington 61274

LNER no. 1274 was the first B1 Class locomotive to enter traffic from the NBLC after Nationalisation, but the engine was still painted in the LNER's green passenger livery with LNER on the tender. From November 1948 the livery for new B1 engines became black with red, cream and grey lining and this subsequently became the standard for the class. The locomotive did not receive its BR number until the first general repair was undertaken at Darlington between 17 January and 2 March 1950. Darlington was also responsible for fitting Automatic Train Control equipment to the locomotive during a general repair that took place between 19 September and 21 October 1958; the equipment is visible here. No. 61274 left service from Wakefield shed in November 1964.

Arthington 46498

Pausing at Arthington station with the 5.28 p.m. service from Leeds to Ilkley is Ivatt Class 2MT no. 46498. The first station at Arthington was opened by the Leeds & Thirsk Railway on 10 July 1849 and was initially named Pool, but renaming had occurred by 1852. In the late 1850s the NER and MR were approached by local residents to build a railway that served Otley and Ilkley and this was agreed to, with the Act being incorporated in 1861. Arthington station had to be re-sited for the opening of the line and it was open to passengers on 1 February 1865. No. 46498 was built at Darlington in February 1952 and its first allocation was to Leeds Holbeck shed. A transfer did not occur until March 1963 when the Scottish Region was reached with an allocation to Motherwell. The remainder of the locomotive's career was spent at various Scottish sheds and the engine left service in September 1965 and was subsequently scrapped.

Opposite above: **Arthington 60074**

No. 60074 *Harvester* is passing Arthington North signal box. It was photographed a year after the previous image of the engine was taken, and a couple of alterations have occurred in the intervening period. Between 5 February and 20 March 1959 a fresh boiler (no. 27041 from no. 60065 *Knight of Thistle*) and a double chimney were fitted during a general repair at Doncaster Works. *Harvester* was a long-term resident at Neville Hill shed having arrived from Gateshead in February 1949, the allocation being broken temporarily by a month working from York at the end of 1950. The locomotive is seen heading 'The Queen of Scots' Pullman service, which operated between London King's Cross, Edinburgh and Glasgow from 1928 until 1964. No. 60074 was withdrawn from Neville Hill in April 1963.

Opposite below: **Alne 60013**

Alne station was opened on 31 March 1841 by the Great North of England Railway and was on the company's line between York and Darlington. In 1891 the station had a bay platform added for the Easingwold branch line. Alne was open for passengers until 5 May 1958 and for freight until 10 August 1964; the land was subsequently cleared. Gresley A4 Class no. 60013 *Dominion of New Zealand* hurtles through the station with 'The Elizabethan' express passenger service during August 1959, which was renamed in 1953 from 'The Capitals Limited' for the Coronation. The service operated until the early 1960s. *Dominion of New Zealand* was a long-term King's Cross shed resident and was withdrawn from there in April 1963.

Hunslet Ballast Cleaner
In May 1961 the Hunslet Engine Co. Ltd, Leeds, completed this track ballast-cleaning apparatus, which was destined for the North Eastern Region of British Rail. The machine could travel at a rate of 600 yards per hour and was self-propelled. Up to 300 tons of stone ballast could be cleaned by the equipment in an hour.

Track Layer
Thomas Smith & Sons Ltd of Rodley, Leeds, were the manufacturers of this new track-laying machine in 1964, which was to be used by the London Midland Region of BR. The firm had been in business in the city from the 1820s and from the 1840s began to specialise in steam-powered cranes. The company was taken over by Northern Engineering Industries in the late 1970s and closed soon after.

Leeds Central Station D9005

British Rail Class 55 diesel-electric locomotive D9005 *The Prince of Wales's Own Regiment of Yorkshire* is seen at Leeds Central station with a passenger service bound for the North East. D9005 was initially based in that area, arriving at Gateshead after it had been built by the Vulcan Foundry in May 1961. Twenty-two were eventually in traffic and all were named after either racehorses or army regiments depending on the region allocated. D9005 acquired its name during a ceremony at York station in October 1963 and just over eleven years later the locomotive was renumbered 55 004. It left service in February 1981 and was then scrapped at Doncaster Works, which cut fifteen other Class 55s; six have been preserved. The stone building behind the first carriage is one of two wagon lifts installed by the Lancashire & Yorkshire Railway and the London & North Western Railway to serve the goods yards around the station. The lifts were operational until the 1950s.

Ferrybridge D1767

In October 1965 Ferrybridge C power station was four months away from producing electricity. It was the third station to be built at the site after Ferrybridge B in the 1950s and Ferrybridge A in the 1920s. Ferrybridge C was capable of producing 2,000 megawatts, which was a significant increase over its predecessors, and in doing so required 800 tons of coal per hour. Ready to satisfy Ferrybridge power station's needs was this Class 47 diesel-electric locomotive, D1767, which was based at Leeds Holbeck shed between July 1965 and September 1966. It had been built by Brush Traction, Loughborough, in October 1964, and was one of many fitted with slow speed control that allowed it to collect and deliver coal using the new 'merry-go-round' system. Seen behind the locomotive are the new 'Hop AB 33' hopper wagons, which were designed for this method.

Leeds City Station 60019

Gresley A4 Pacific no. 60019 *Bittern* had only just entered its retirement when this picture was taken in November 1966, which sees it still hard at work operating a special Railway Correspondence and Travel Society service. The locomotive is seen setting off from Leeds City station with 'The Waverley' service that would take it to Carlisle and Edinburgh. The locomotive was housed at Leeds Neville Hill shed in the late 1960s, where it awaited restoration, but a number of other moves followed, as well as changes in ownership, before no. 60019 returned to steam in 2007.

Leeds City Station 60019
Deltic locomotive no. *55 019 Royal Highland Fusilier* is pictured in Leeds City station on 4 June 1974 and illustrated a *Yorkshire Evening Post* article of 19 June 1974 detailing a recruitment drive for train drivers: 'British Rail direct recruitment for engine drivers could mean the unexpected realisation of boyhood dreams for many men,' said the newspaper, adding, 'A ride in the cab of a crack express represents the summit of a driver's career.' Formerly D9019, the locomotive was withdrawn on 31 December 1981 and acquired by the Deltic Preservation Society. The DPS website states: 'D9019 entered service on December 29th 1961, based at Haymarket depot in Edinburgh, and received her Royal Highland Fusilier nameplates at a ceremony in Glasgow in September 1965. Renumbered 55019 in November 1973, the loco was one of only five members of the class to undergo and extensive general overhaul, this being carried out during an eight month visit to Doncaster Works. 55019 was withdrawn on December 31st 1981, after hauling the 16.30 Aberdeen–York between Edinburgh and York – this was the final BR Deltic hauled service train. It was therefore appropriate that the loco should become the first to operate a train in preservation, an event which took place at the North Yorkshire Moors Railway eight months later, on August 22nd 1982. The locomotive remained on the NYMR until 1987, when she moved to the Midland Railway Centre and later the Great Central Railway.'

Leeds City Station 55 002
The end of an era occurred on 5 May 1978 as all but one Pullman service was to be stopped by British Rail. 'The Yorkshire Pullman' service between Harrogate and King's Cross had been in operation since the 1930s and appropriately Class 55 no. No. 55 002 *King's Own Yorkshire Light Infantry* is seen heading the final service to the capital. Built by the Vulcan Foundry in March 1961, the locomotive was not named until April 1963 in a ceremony at York. The name had previously been in the possession of LNER V2 Class 2-6-2 locomotive no. 4843, BR no. 60872. 55 002 was withdrawn in January 1982 and subsequently preserved by the National Railway Museum.

Penistone 76025

In the mid-1930s a scheme to electrify the line between Wath, Sheffield and Manchester was set in motion by the LNER and a prototype electric locomotive, LNER no. 6701, was constructed at Doncaster Works in 1941 to a design produced by Gresley. However, at the start of the Second World War the electrification was put on hold and not resurrected until after Nationalisation. The line was electrified gradually with the first section ready in 1952 and the line completed in January 1955. BR built a fleet of electric locomotives based on Gresley's prototype to work the line; between 1950 and 1953, fifty-seven locomotives, classified EM1 (later BR Class 76), were constructed at Gorton. Several larger locomotives that were classified EM2 (BR Class 77) were also constructed at the Works between 1953 and 1954. Passenger services were only in operation until 5 January 1970, however, when coal and freight traffic took over its use. A further ten years elapsed before the line was scheduled to close completely on 18 July 1981. No. 76 025, built at Gorton in January 1952 as no. 26 025, is seen at Penistone station on 21 April 1981 with the Locomotive Club of Great Britain's 'Easter Tommy' rail tour, which was the final passenger service on the line, running between Rotherwood Sidings and Guide Bridge. No. 76 025 was withdrawn in July 1981 and subsequently scrapped, but one class member – no. 76 020 – has been preserved by the NRM.

Rotherham Masbrough Nuclear Waste

On 29 September 1981 this Class 47 diesel-electric locomotive, no. 47 134, was photographed with a train of nuclear waste passing through Rotherham Masbrough station. As may have been predicted, these 'nuclear' train journeys through South Yorkshire caused extreme concern in the area and were monitored closely by anti-nuclear groups. It was believed that most of the trains began their journeys at various naval bases in the south of England. The final destination was the nuclear processing plant at Windscale, Cumbria. The container carrying the waste by the 'Rotherham' train was about 10 ft in length, cylindrical and suspended upright in the trailer which was claimed to be a missile carrier, but which the manufacturer said was designed for transporting nuclear submarine fuel. In the bottom picture, note the observation post at the end of the carriage and the box-shaped cooling device on the trailer. Attached to the carriage are metal rods which could be used to 'sniff out' radiation leaks.

York Holgate Bridge
The *Yorkshire Post* reported on 31 October 1985 that Holgate Bridge, York, was causing a problem for the east coast main line electrification scheme as it was too low and BR were considering raising it. The bridge had been replaced twice previously because of expansion of the lines to York station in 1877 and in 1911 to allow tram services to operate over it. The electrification of the line began in 1985 and the first section to be operational was between King's Cross and Leeds in 1988. Completion occurred in 1990.

West Yorkshire Passenger Transport Executive Super Sprinter
In the late 1980s this BR Class 155 Super Sprinter DMU was constructed by British Leyland to replace first-generation DMUs (like the one seen on the right) that were reaching the end of their operational life. No. 155 341 was one of several that were built for the West Yorkshire Passenger Transport Executive in 1988 for local services. Forty-two trainsets were produced in total and they consisted of two coaches, DMSL and DMS, with a Cummins NT855-R5 285-hp diesel engine. The length of the carriages was 76 ft 5 in. and seating was provided for a total of 156 passengers (DMSL-76, DMS-80).

Gascoigne Wood 56123
On 25 September 1987 this image was taken of British Railways Class 56 diesel-electric locomotive no. 56123 collecting a load of 1,000 tons of coal from Gascoigne Wood Colliery, Selby, which was destined for a power station in the local area. The colliery was the focal point for coal production in the Selby coalfield and received the coal that was mined from five pits in the area – North Selby, Riccall, Stillingfleet, Whitemoor and Wistow. A conveyor belt 14,000 metres long, which was supplied by Cable Belt Ltd at a cost of £15 million, brought coal to the surface at 20 mph and deposited it in outloading bunkers. The coal was then deposited into hopper wagons and a 1,000-ton load could be ready in half an hour. No. 56 123 was erected at Crewe in July 1983 and was in service until August 2003.

Class 155 Super Sprinter 155 303
Thirty-five of the Class 155 trainsets have since been split into seventy one-carriage trains and re-classified Class 153. This was undertaken by Hunslet-Barclay, Kilmarnock, between 1991 and 1992, and the main changes concerned the cab. Seating was reduced to between 69-72, depending on the operating company, and the weight was increased to 41.2 tons. The Class 155 trainsets made for the West Yorkshire Passenger Transport Executive are still at work in their original form in the West Yorkshire area.

Leeds Station
On 11 March 1989 the first electric train ran from King's Cross station to Leeds on the newly electrified east coast main line; it is seen here arriving at platform 5A.

Leeds Station – New Class 158
Arriving at Leeds station in January 1991 with a service from Liverpool Lime Street station is a Class 158 Express Sprinter DMU. The class was the product of Derby Works and 182 trainsets entered service between 1989 and 1992. The majority featured two carriages, but seventeen of the class were three-coach sets. Three variations of engine existed and 158 736 was fitted with a Cummins NT855R diesel engine in each car, which developed 350 hp. The final ten Class 158s, nos 158 901-158 910, were built specifically for West Yorkshire Passenger Transport Executive with slight detail alterations. No. 158 736 has since moved to Scotland and works in the Edinburgh area.

Bedale Station 37 714
The line between Northallerton and Garsdale was opened in stages between the late 1840s and the late 1870s by the York, Newcastle & Berwick Railway and its successor the North Eastern Railway. When completed the line joined the east coast main line with the Settle and Carlisle line and was fully operational until April 1954 when it closed for passengers. Subsequently the track was lifted between Redmire and Garsdale, but the section between Northallerton and Redmire remained active for mineral traffic. At the end of 1992 this function ceased and the last train to Redmire was hauled by Class 37 no. 37 714 and an unidentified class member, seen here passing Bedale station. However, the Ministry of Defence stepped in and retained the line to move men and materials between Catterick Garrison, and from the mid-2000s the Wensleydale Railway have operated the line.

Redmire 60 030
Passing Redmire station during February 1992 with a train of mineral wagons bound for a nearby limestone quarry is this BR Class 60 diesel-electric locomotive. No. 60 030 was erected at Brush Traction Ltd, Loughborough, in November 1990 as part of an order from BR's Trainload Freight division; the locomotive has the metal sub-division livery applied in this photograph. A total of 100 locomotives were produced by Brush Traction between 1989 and 1993. The photograph was taken around the time of a controversial proposal from British Steel to transport limestone dust from Redmire Quarry, near Leyburn, to Teeside, by road instead of rail.

CHAPTER 2

Marshalling Yards
Sheds and Works

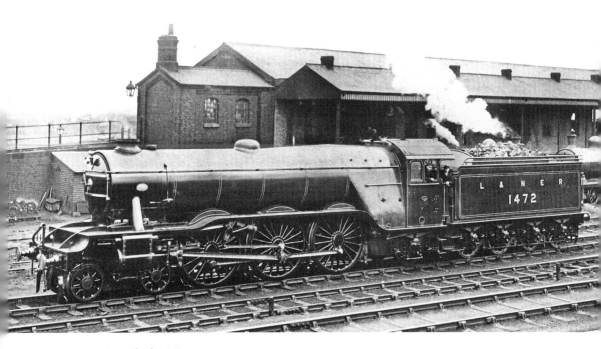

Doncaster Carr Shed 1472
No. 1472 was the first A1 Class Pacific locomotive to enter traffic for the LNER from Doncaster Works and is pictured here not long after it was completed in February 1923. The location is Doncaster Carr shed and in the background is the north coal stage. The original north coal stage had been built with the shed in 1876, but it was reconstructed on the same site in 1898 to include a driver's room, which was located underneath the stage. Messrs. Arnold & Sons completed the work for £3,668 and in later years the coal stage lost the canopy seen here. The name *Flying Scotsman* was given to the locomotive in February 1924 and a month later the engine was given its LNER number – 4472. Note that 'L&NER' and '1472' have been applied on the tender.

Doncaster Carr Shed
During the late 1920s Doncaster Carr shed underwent a number of improvements with one of them being the provision of a mechanical coaler that had a capacity of 500 tons. It replaced the southern coal stage, which was removed. The north stage, however, was retained for use if the need arose. The photograph dates from *c.* 1937.

Kitson & Co. Steam and Diesel Locomotive

This odd-looking locomotive was constructed by Leeds company Kitson & Co. in the late 1920s and featured a combined steam and diesel engine that was designed by William Still. The engine had eight cylinders that were double acting – meaning the cylinder was powered at one end by diesel and at the other end by steam. To produce the necessary steam, a small boiler was heated by burning oil before the exhaust was utilised for the task. Then, once a set speed was reached the 2-6-2T locomotive would use only diesel power. The LNER used the locomotive on a number of trials, as well as some regular services, basing the engine at Leeds and then York. Kitson & Co. invested a large amount of money into the venture and it was partially to blame for the company entering receivership in the early 1930s. The locomotive was returned to Kitson & Co. to be scrapped in 1935 and the company had gone out of business by the end of the decade.

Leeds Holbeck Shed

An unidentified locomotive returns to Holbeck shed in this picture taken from Nineveh Road in May 1958. The shed building, containing two roundhouses, was constructed by the Midland Railway in May 1868 and a repair shop and ramped coal stage were also installed at this time. A LMS no. 1-type mechanical coaler with a 300 ton capacity was the only major addition to the site during its life as a steam shed. In the final months of 1967 the shed closed to steam and the mechanical coaler was demolished during May 1969.

Opposite below: **Leeds Neville Hill 62744**

Neville Hill shed was opened by the NER during October 1894 on the north side of the line to Selby. The building contained four roundhouses, but this was later reduced to two by BR in 1960. Gresley D49/2 Class 4-4-0 no. 62744 *The Holderness* was erected at Darlington Works in October 1932 and entered traffic as LNER no. 273. It is seen at Neville Hill during November 1951 after being coaled. The locomotive has a Group Standard tender with stepped-out side sheets, which could carry 4,200 gallons of water and 7½ tons of coal. Withdrawal occurred in December 1960.

Leeds Neville Hill 60084

This Gresley A3 Class locomotive was built at Doncaster Works in February 1930 and commenced work as LNER no. 2595 *Trigo*. The engine was the first to receive a new type non-corridor tender, no. 5476, and it was carried by the locomotive until it was removed at a General repair in October 1940. A streamlined non-corridor tender, no. 5645, replaced no. 5476 and was paired with the engine until no. 60084's withdrawal in November 1964. *Trigo* was allocated to Neville Hill shed from September 1949 to December 1963 when it returned to Gateshead, which was the locomotive's residence for a large portion of its early career.

Leeds Neville Hill 60126

Peppercorn A1 Class Pacific no. 60126 *Sir Vincent Raven* had been in traffic two years and seven months when this photograph was taken at Neville Hill shed on 27 November 1951. The locomotive was allocated to Heaton shed at this time and had been there since the start of its career. Leeds was a regular destination for Peppercorn A1s at Heaton and they could also work between York and Edinburgh, with a regular diagram also taking them to Grantham. *Sir Vincent Raven* only made one transfer to York, which occurred in September 1961 and the locomotive was withdrawn from there in January 1965.

Leeds Copley Hill 60139

Darlington-built Peppercorn A1 no. 60139 *Sea Eagle* is illustrated here in Copley Hill shed's yard. The engine was constructed in December 1948 and was named in May 1950. A4 Class Pacific no. 4487 had previously been named *Sea Eagle*, but it became *Walter K. Whigham* in October 1947. Copley Hill saw twenty members of the Peppercorn A1 Class reside at the shed between 1950 and September 1964 when it closed to traffic; no. 60139 arrived from King's Cross in July 1951 and left for Grantham in December 1955. Peppercorn A1 no. 60141 *Abbotsford* can be seen outside Copley Hill shed to the right in the picture. *Sea Eagle* was condemned in June 1964.

Opposite below: **Leeds Neville Hill 60539**

Waiting by the mechanical coaler at Neville Hill shed is Peppercorn A2 Class Pacific no. 60539 *Bronzino*. The locomotive was the last of fifteen to be built at Doncaster and entered service at the end of August 1948. *Bronzino* was the only class member to carry a double chimney from new, although a further five engines received the arrangement in 1949. No. 60539 was allocated to Heaton and Tweedmouth during its life and was withdrawn from the latter in November 1962. Neville Hill's mechanical coaler was built in the early 1930s by the Mitchell Conveyor and Transporter Co. Ltd for close to £8,000.

Leeds Copley Hill 61246
Thompson B1 4-6-0 no. 61246 *Lord Balfour of Burleigh* was one of eighteen class members to receive the name of a LNER director between November and December 1947. The locomotive had been constructed by the NBLC in October and was based at Doncaster at the time of naming. Transferred to Scotland in September 1953, no. 61246 spent the rest of its career based in the country working from St Margaret's shed (two spells) and Dalry Road shed. The locomotive was cut up at Cowlairs Works after leaving service in December 1962.

York North Shed 60146 and 61454
A view from York North shed's mechanical coaler shows Peppercorn A1 Class no. 60146 *Peregrine* arriving to be coaled and Raven B16 Class 4-6-0 no. 61454. No. 60146 entered traffic from Darlington Works in April 1949 and was named in December 1950. Like no. 60139, the locomotive received a discarded name, with *Peregrine* previously being used by A4 no. 4903, BR no. 60034, which became *Lord Faringdon* in March 1948. No. 61454 was also erected at Darlington, but the date of completion was September 1923. Both engines were residents of York shed when this picture was taken on 29 December 1952. Of interest to the left of no. 60146 are two NER snow ploughs.

Opposite below: **Leeds Copley Hill 60826**
Also in Copley Hill shed's yard is Gresley V2 Class no. 60826, which was erected at Darlington in January 1928 as LNER no. 4797. The pony truck originally fitted to the class was of Gresley's design, using swing link side control suspension. However, at the end of the Second World War it was discovered, after a series of mishaps involving the class, that Gresley's pony truck was adversely affected by the poor condition of the country's track. It was deemed necessary to substitute the pony truck with a new design that incorporated spring side control suspension, which was in use on a number of Thompson's classes at the time. Alteration of the V2 Class began in November 1948 and was concluded in April 1952. No. 60826 was altered at an unknown date, but is noticeable here due to a lack of front guard irons attached to the main frames as well as short cylinder drainpipes.

York Carriage and Wagon Works

The finishing touches are applied to a BR AM2 Electric Multiple Unit at York Carriage and Wagon Works in February 1959. Doncaster Works also produced some of the four carriage sets and between the two Works 112 sets were constructed from 1958 to 1960. York had to employ extra electricians to build the sets as approximately two miles of intricate wiring was present in each carriage and roughly 800 employees were involved in all aspects of the building work. The EMUs were intended to work on London Liverpool Street to Southend services and 363 passengers could be carried. The sets later became BR Class 302 under the TOPS scheme.

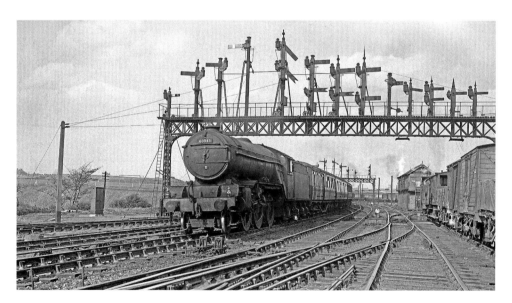

Leeds Neville Hill 60843

After being built at Darlington in December 1938, the initial allocation of no. 60843 was to York shed. The locomotive was based there when this photograph was taken during May 1953, which shows no. 60843 at Neville Hill, Leeds, with a Newcastle to Leeds passenger service. The engine did have brief spells at Neville Hill shed and Copley Hill shed during the mid-1940s and late 1950s respectively. No. 60843 was sent to J. Cashmore, Great Bridge, to be scrapped after being withdrawn from Ardsley in October 1965. Visible to the right is Neville Hill East signal box.

Hunslet Austerity Conversion

During the Second World War the War Department selected the Hunslet Engine Company's 50550 Class 0-6-0ST design for construction to meet their shunting needs. In total 377 were built at a number of Works and these later found a variety of homes after the war. Ninety were retained by the forces and were used by them up to the 1960s when some were sold to the National Coal Board. This unidentified locomotive is being modified by Hunslet before being entering service for the NCB. The main alteration was the fitting of an underfeed stoker with new grate and firebox layout to reduce emissions as a result of the Clean Air Act. The photograph was taken in 1963.

Tinsley Traction Maintenance Depot

On 24 June 1964 this view of the new Traction Maintenance Depot at Tinsley, Sheffield, was taken. Twelve roads were present in the building, split evenly between each end with a total capacity of twenty-four locomotives. In the middle of the structure was an area for machining equipment and parts storage and this separated the maintenance tracks from extending through the building. Almost all types of repairs could be undertaken at the depot with the exception of engine removal as there were no overhead cranes provided. The depot was closed in 1998 and the site has been re-utilised for the erection of offices.

Tinsley Marshalling Control

A view inside the control room at Tinsley Marshalling Yard on 29 September 1965. The *Sheffield Star* of 1 November of the same year said that dozens of families had visited the marshalling yard on the previous day for a tour and inspection of the yard and the diesel maintenance depot. Wives and families of men employed by British Railways at the yard travelled to Tinsley in a special train. During the afternoon, there was a demonstration of 'hump shunting', showing the use of the unique Dowty equipment in the removal of railway wagons. Mr F. Harrison, divisional movements manager of the British Railways Eastern Region, explained the workings of the shunting, which had been installed in a marshalling yard for the first time ever.

Tinsley Marshalling Yard Opening

A study of the railway system in the Sheffield area during the late 1950s and early 1960s brought about proposals for a single-engine shed, one freight depot (to replace the nine in use at the time), and a new marshalling yard. Grimesthorpe was chosen to be the location of the freight depot, on the site of the old steam shed, while the locomotive shed and marshalling yard were both located at Tinsley. The marshalling yard was officially opened on 29 October 1965 by the former Chairman of BR Lord Beeching, pictured here unveiling the plaque. The *Sheffield Star* of that day said a special train had left the city's Victoria station for a 6-mile journey to the world's most modern railway marshalling yard and freight terminal. On board was Lord Beeching with 250 top railway and industrial 'brass'. Lord Beeching said, 'This is a significant day for Sheffield and British Railways.'

Tinsley Marshalling Yard

A view of Tinsley Marshalling Yard looking north during September 1965. On the right is the control tower, while on the left is the diesel locomotive service shed. A BR Class 20 diesel-electric locomotive, D8066, is also seen, entering the scene from the right. With the decline of rail traffic in the 1970s and 1980s, Tinsley Marshalling Yard was wound down and sections of the track have been progressively lifted.

Tinsley Marshalling Yard Signal Box
The state-of-the-art controls in Tinsley Yard signal box in September 1965. The *Sheffield Star* of 29 October 1965 said that the huge marshalling yard was handling 3,000 wagons a day and had the capacity for another thousand, adding that it received or dispatched a train every five minutes.

Doncaster Works E3140
After a number of prototype AC electric locomotives were built in the late 1950s and early 1960s, a production batch of 100 locomotives was commissioned and completed between 1965 and 1966. Doncaster Works and Vulcan Foundry constructed forty and sixty respectively and the locomotives were classified AL6, later becoming BR Class 86. This locomotive was the last of the order to be constructed at Doncaster and is pictured at the Works on 18 January 1966.

Wath Marshalling Yard

A marshalling yard at Wath-upon-Dearne was opened by the Great Central Railway in 1907 to handle coal from the many collieries in the area. The yard was of the 'hump' type where gravity was used to sort the coal wagons into trains instead of shunting locomotives. However, a number of powerful engines were on hand in case they were needed, such as the GCR 8H Class 0-8-4T engines or the LNER U1 Class Beyer Garratt 2-8-0+0-8-2. By 23 February 1968, the date of this picture, steam locomotives had been ousted and BR Class 37s had replaced them; D6706, D6709 and an unidentified class member are present in the yard.

Wath Marshalling Yard

On the 29 December 1987 a completely different image of Wath Marshalling Yard has been captured. The land remains derelict and awaiting re-development.

Neville Hill Carriage Sidings
A panoramic scene at Neville Hill including the carriage sidings, taken on 24 March 1969 from the west end. The centre building was for cleaning and servicing, while the one to the left in the foreground was for DMU servicing. In the left background (from left to right) are the shed, diesel locomotive servicing building and diesel locomotive repair shop.

Neville Hill Carriage Sidings
Another view of Neville Hill's carriage sidings, but from the east end. This picture also dates from early 1969 and features the east end control cabin in the foreground. Neville Hill shed became the focal point for diesel locomotives and coaching stock in the Leeds area at the end of steam traction as all but Holbeck shed had closed during the mid-1960s. Neville Hill retains this function to this day. Holbeck shed closed during 1986 only to be reopened by Northern Rail in 2006.

Neville Hill Carriage Sidings
A DMU passes through the wash plant at Neville Hill carriage sidings in the late 1960s. The wash plant used 350 gallons of water a minute to remove the dirt and grime that had been accumulated during service. Neville Hill East Signal Box is seen on the left of the photograph.

Doncaster Works 532
Peppercorn A2 Class Pacific no. 60532 *Blue Peter* was withdrawn from service by BR on 31 December 1966 while allocated to Aberdeen Ferryhill shed. The locomotive was then stored for a time before being bought by Geoff Drury. Funds were required for the locomotive's restoration and after a public appeal, aided by the BBC Television programme of the same name, *Blue Peter* entered Doncaster Works in May 1969. No. 60532 underwent a light overhaul and was repainted before a renaming ceremony (depicted here) on 22 November 1970. The locomotive has LNER on the tender and is numbered 532 – two features that the engine never had when it was in service.

Neville Hill Carriage Depot

Two examiners at Neville Hill Carriage Depot examine a BR single-bolster bogie during early 1973. BR designed two types of bogies for its coaching stock: one for local passenger and parcel coaches and a strengthened bogie for kitchen and sleeping carriages. This bogie is attached to a diagram 126-corridor composite coach, which was one of 1,268 constructed between 1951 and 1963 by a variety of manufacturers. Twenty-four seats, split between four compartments, were available in first class, while eighteen second class seats were present and divided into three compartments. The carriage was 64 ft 6 in. long by 9 ft 3 in. wide, and the first and second class compartments measured 7 ft 2 in. long and 6 ft 3 in. long respectively.

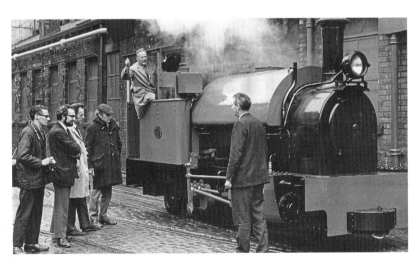

Hunslet Last Locomotive

This locomotive marked the end of an era when it was completed by the Hunslet Engine Co. in November 1971. It was the last steam engine built by the company and the final steam engine for industrial use to be erected in Britain. The 0-4-2ST engine, built to the 'Brazil' design that had originated at Kerr, Stuart & Co., was to be exported to Java to work at the Trangkil Sugar Mill and as a result became Trangkil no. 4. In 2004 the locomotive was repatriated to Britain and re-gauged to work in preservation at the Statfold Barn Railway. Mr Raymond Woodhead, who was Foreman Erector at the Hunslet Engine Co., is pictured in the cab of the locomotive after its completion.

Hudswell Clarke & Co. Ltd Underground Locomotive
After the Hunslet Engine Co. took over Hudswell Clarke & Co. Ltd in 1973 it was decided to continue production at the Works and this 100-hp underground locomotive was the latest product. It had been ordered by the NCB and was destined for Cynheidre Colliery, Wales. The company were hoping that their design of colliery locomotive would be adopted by the new complex serving the Selby coalfield, the *Yorkshire Evening Post* noted on 14 May 1976. Sinking operations at Selby had just begun and a spokesman for Hudswell Clarke & Co. Ltd said, 'Obviously we are now looking at Selby very closely.'

Hunslet Shunting Locomotive
The *Yorkshire Post* of 11 December 1978 reported that a handing over ceremony for the first Hunslet 0-8-0 shunting locomotive to be completed for an order by the newly formed Kenya Railways had taken place. A total of fifteen were to be completed by the Hunslet Engine Co., with a further twenty to be erected by British Rail Engineering Ltd (BREL) Swindon Works using wheelsets, gearboxes and other components supplied by Hunslet.

Doncaster New Erecting Shop
A scene in the New Erecting (E2) Shop at Doncaster Works. In the background is a Doncaster-built BR Class 58 diesel-electric locomotive no. 58 012, which was erected during March 1984.

Doncaster Station
Five hundred workers from Doncaster Works travelled to Derby for a rally on 10 August 1984, and some members of the NUR no. 3 branch are seen here outside Doncaster station.

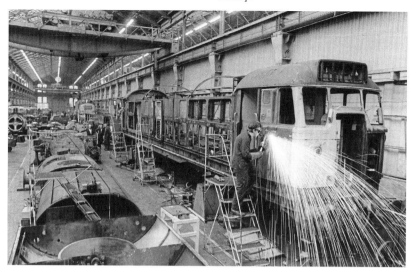

Doncaster Crimpsall Repair Shop

Pictured in bay no. 2 at Doncaster Works' Crimpsall Repair Shop on 3 January 1984 is a stripped down and unidentified Class 31 diesel-electric locomotive. The 263 locomotives of the class were originally built by Brush Traction between 1957 and 1962 as Class 30 and featured a Mirlees JVS12T engine. However, in service a number of cracks appeared in the welds in the engine and it was eventually decided to replace the Mirlees units with an English Electric 12SVT 1,470-hp engine. The task was completed in 1969 resulting in the re-classification.

Doncaster Works Paint Shop

The Class 56 locomotives were built to work heavy freight services and coal traffic. One hundred and thirty-five in total were built by three Works: Electroputere (Romania) – 30; Doncaster Works – 85; and Crewe Works – 20. No. 56 031, pictured here in the Doncaster Paint Shop, was the first to be erected at Doncaster and entered traffic in April 1977, while the last of the class was completed at Crewe in November 1984. Not all of the construction necessary for the Class 56 locomotives was performed at Doncaster, and a number of other BREL Works were involved in constructing parts for the locomotives. At the time of writing no. 56 031 is still in service.

Left: **Doncaster Works Paint Shop**
The last Class 58 diesel-electric locomotive, no. 58 050, to be built at Doncaster Works receives its livery from painter Malcolm Standege in the Paint Shop on 26 January 1987. The Paint Shop was built in around 1900 and it had eight roads with shallow pits, with the east end of the building used to store and mix paint. From the mid-1930s the Paint Shop housed the Works' compressed air equipment, which consisted of three 750-cu.-ft-capacity compressors attached to 157-hp electric motors. In 1987 locomotives began to be painted in the Crimpsall Repair Shop and the Paint Shop was used for storage. Both buildings have since been demolished.

Right: **Doncaster Works**
Employees of Doncaster Works leave the site using this footbridge over the east coast main line on 21 May 1986.

Doncaster Crimpsall Repair Shop 37 220
In the Crimpsall Repair Shop at Doncaster Works at the opposite end to the unidentified Class 31, is this Class 37 diesel-electric locomotive. It was constructed at Vulcan Foundry in January 1964 and was in service until August 2005. The Crimpsall Repair Shop was completed in around 1901 for the Great Northern Railway at a cost of £294,000. It contained four large repair bays that were 520 ft long by 52 ft wide and two smaller bays of 30 ft wide for use by the workforce.

York Carriage and Wagon Works
Two representatives from the West Yorkshire Passenger Transport Executive view a BR Class 321 EMU at York Carriage and Wagon Works in February 1990. Two batches of sixty-six and forty-eight trainsets were initially built at the Works between 1988 and 1990 before the final batch of three were constructed for the WYPTE in 1991. Classified 321/9, the EMUs were built to work on the line between Leeds and Doncaster and are currently still at work on the route, having been refurbished in the mid-2000s. The trainsets are made up of four carriages, with the formation being DTSO-MSO-TSOL-DTSO, and seating is provided for 307 passengers.

CHAPTER 3
Ceremonies

York 'Tubeliner'
Tracy Talbot waves the flag for driver Dave Smith to set off from York station with a load of steel coils bound for Corby in the East Midlands on 29 September 1982. The train had stopped in York to commemorate BR moving 750,000 tons of steel in the previous eighteen months between Corby and Lackenby Steel Works, Teesside. Mr Frank Paterson, general manager of BR's North Eastern Region, told the *Yorkshire Post* that the trains were taking the strain off Britain's roads as 45,000 lorries would have been required to complete the task of the 'Tubeliner' trains.

Leeds City Station 141 006
Trumpeters from the 1st Battalion, The King's Own Royal Border Regiment, heralded the arrival of this new BR Class 141 'Pacer' diesel railbus to Leeds City station on 19 March 1984. It was the first of twenty-two two-car sets that had been ordered by the WYPTE at a cost of £350,000 each from British Leyland. The chairman of the West Yorkshire County Council, County Councillor William Sykes (right) is seen with a silver salver that was presented to him by the chairman of BR, Mr Bob Reid (left), to mark the arrival of the locomotive.

North Yorkshire Moors Railway 45428
LMS Stanier Class 5 or 'Black Five' 4-6-0 no. 45428 was built by Armstrong Whitworth & Co. Ltd during October 1937. Three-hundred-and-twenty-seven were constructed by the company for the LMS between April 1935 and December 1937. After no. 45428's career came to an end in October 1967, when it was withdrawn from Leeds Holbeck shed, it subsequently found its way into preservation on the North Yorkshire Moors Railway. On 8 April 1985 no. 45428 acquired the name *Eric Treacy* after the late Bishop of Wakefield, also a keen railway photographer and enthusiast, who had died at Appleby station on 13 May 1978. Making the engine shine for its first journey with the name is driver Howard Smith and fireman Mike Oliver.

Sprinter Link

The Sprinter, BR's replacement for the old DMUs, was given a champagne send off at Sheffield Midland Railway station on 8 August 1985 by Miss Sprinter Trophy, Vanessa Mooney, of York. At that time it was predicted that the train would first enter regular service on the Nottingham-Sheffield-Leeds line. The *Sheffield Star* of 20 November 1984 had said that the Sprinter was powered by a new generation of diesel engines, which BR claimed cut maintenance by one-third, reduced fuel consumption and reduced journey times by about 10 per cent. 'BR has earmarked £360m to replace all the ageing diesel multiple units on its provincial services by 1990,' claimed the newspaper, adding 'The new Sprinter ... carries 138 passengers ... Each two-coach unit costs £500,000 ... BR believes the efficiency of the new Sprinter could save some lines threatened with closure, as well as helping meet Government demands for cuts in railway subsidies ... BR has ordered 50 of the new trains ... and is hoping the Government will then give the go-ahead for another 120.'

Ferrybridge 56 089

This Class 56 locomotive, no. 56 089, received the name *Ferrybridge C Power Station* in September 1991 during a ceremony at Ferrybridge C power station at Knottingley, West Yorkshire. Powergen Chief Executive Ed Wallace, pictured, bestowed the name on the locomotive, which had been built at Doncaster in January 1981. The naming ceremony coincided with an open weekend to celebrate the power station's 25th anniversary.

Sheffield Midland Railway Station

During late April 1987 the *Sheffield Star* announced that the start of British Rail's summer timetable on May 11 of that year would herald the introduction of new trains on South Yorkshire rail services. Sprinters were to go into service on the Sheffield–Doncaster–Cleethorpes service. Later they were to be used on the Sheffield–Doncaster–Hull service. With the introduction of the trains, BR hoped the Sprinters would set new standards of comfort with their double-glazed tinted windows, sliding doors and spacious interiors. The Sprinter was designed to provide a quiet getaway and fast acceleration with a top speed of 75 mph. Sprinter 150 228 is pictured with members of South Yorkshire Transport Committee on 29 April 1987. They are, from left to right: Brian Surtees, Richard Parkins, Ian Smith and Jack Meredith.

CHAPTER 4
Rail Crashes

Thirsk Rail Crash DP2

On 31 July 1967 the 12.00 p.m. King's Cross to Edinburgh express collided with a cement wagon at approximately 50 mph on the down fast line near Thirsk. The wagon had become detached from the partially derailed Cliffe to Uddingston cement train, which had BR Class 40 D283 at the helm and was travelling on the down slow line. Tragically seven people were killed in the accident and forty-five were injured; the driver and second man of the express luckily escaped serious injury. DP2, an English Electric Type Four prototype, was built at Vulcan Foundry in 1962 and was withdrawn as a result of the collision.

Thirsk Rail Crash
These mangled cement wagons and passenger carriages were involved in the collision near Thirsk on 31 July 1967. The derailment of the cement wagon was blamed on worn suspension that caused it to jump off the track. Subsequently new speed restrictions were placed on the wagons.

Thirsk Rail Crash
Police gather some of the belongings strewn onto the track after the crash at Thirsk. The violence of the collision is clearly illustrated from the damage caused to the carriage, which was the first behind the locomotive.

Cornholme Derailed Wagon
Mrs Rita Shaw of Oakley Terrace, Cornholme, had a rude awakening on 16 August 1967 when this goods wagon was derailed and crashed into the side of her house while she was in bed. The wagon had come off the line between Todmorden and Burnley, which runs through the village.

Stainforth Derailed Tanker
Five naphtha tankers were derailed on the line between Stainforth and Thorne during August 1968. Firemen had to keep a constant watch on the tankers as there was a risk that the volatile liquid gas could explode.

Haxby Level Crossing Collision
The damage to this DMU, on a York to Scarborough service, was caused by a raised crossing gate, which had also hit a car that was on the level crossing at Haxby, near York, on 28 October 1968. The driver of the train, Mr George Craven, was pinned in his cab for forty minutes before he was freed. Fortuitously he was only suffering from shock and the effects of broken glass. The driver and passenger in the car that had hit the gate were uninjured, but understandably shocked.

Goole – Leeds DMU Passenger Train Collision

When a four-coach DMU passenger train smashed into a derailed goods train near the centre of Leeds around noon on 18 April 1969 three people were slightly injured but another twenty escaped unhurt. The collision occurred as the 10.48 a.m. Goole to Leeds passed under a bridge in New Peppar Road, Hunslet. Thirteen goods wagons laden with coal slack peeled off the rails as the passenger train, on the next track, was about to overtake. As passengers scrambled from the wrecked coaches a railway foreman who saw the collision ran 70 yards down the line to raise the alarm and stop other rail traffic. All emergency services were called out, while railwaymen working nearby comforted passengers and made tea for them. As the injured were taken to hospital other passengers were shuttled by taxi to Leeds City station. Only one train was cancelled but there were minor delays to other traffic which was diverted until normal service was resumed two hours later. A British Rail official at the scene of the crash said the coal wagons had knocked the front coach of the passenger train off the line and it travelled at least 60 yards, its wheels tearing into concrete sleepers. At his home hours later, Henry Sherwood, sixty-two, a train driver for twenty years, said he placed detonators on the line to warn other trains while suffering from shock and handicapped by a back injury. He said modestly: 'My only thought was for the safety of my passengers and my train. I only did what was expected of me.'

Thorne Lands End Road Crossing Collision

One man was killed and seven injured when the van in which they were travelling was struck by a train on an unmanned level crossing in Alexandra Street, Thorne, near Doncaster on 25 July 1969. The train was a 4.26 p.m. Doncaster to Hull DMU carrying about 250 passengers. The accident occurred at 4.45 p.m. The driver of the train was treated for head injuries and shock and none of the train passengers were injured. They continued their journey by bus.

Opposite above and below: **Thorne Lands End Road Crossing Collision**

The van involved in the Alexandra St Crossing crash was carried about 20 yards down the track and tossed into a ditch. The vehicle, owned by William Press Ltd of Bawtry, was carrying their workmen who had been engaged on a natural gas conversion job. The crossing, known as Lands End Road crossing, had witnessed two fatal accidents in the previous two years.

Melton Halt Collision
Dense fog was to blame for this collision on Thursday 11 November 1976. A passenger train bound for Goole crashed into the back of a thirty-wagon goods train near Melton Halt, Ferriby, on the Hull to Goole line. Driver Stanley Smith and trainee driver Stephen Cooper were among several people with injuries caused by the accident.

Melton Halt Collision
Another view of the collision near Melton Halt showing the damage caused to the front end of Metropolitan-Cammell Class 101 first generation DMU, DMBS car E51238, and the guards' van at the end of the goods train.

Tinsley Runaway Train
Running away from its duties at Tinsley Marshalling Yard on 21 April 1979 is this BR Class
08 diesel-electric shunting locomotive, no. 08 223, which has almost made it on to Sheffield
Parkway. The shunter had been built at Derby Works in December 1956 and was withdrawn
two months after this crash and later scrapped.

Tinsley Runaways
Three other locomotives in a runaway incident at Tinsley on 5 April 1982 include nos 47 342,
40 007 and 08 482.

Northallerton Derailment
Investigations were underway after all ten carriages from this Intercity 125 train left the track at 70 mph on 28 August 1979 at Northallerton. The 500 passengers that were on the train averted further disaster when a quick-thinking signalman diverted another Intercity 125 that was approaching the stricken train. It was thought the train may have hit something that was on the track.

Tinsley Runaway Trains
A pair of Class 20 diesel-electric locomotives attempt a similar escape from Tinsley Marshalling Yard on 5 August 1981. Thankfully, no one was hurt in the dramatic runaway which was just one of several similar events which occurred at the marshalling yard. The first locomotive is no. 20 022 and it was constructed at the Robert Stephenson & Hawthorn Ltd Works in October 1959 to English Electric's Type One design. Two-hundred-and-twenty-eight were produced at the Works and English Electric's Vulcan Foundry between 1957 and 1968. No. 20 022 was withdrawn in August 1988.

Ulleskelf Derailment
Eighty passengers were involved in a derailment on 8 December 1981 after carriages from the 13.50 p.m. York to Liverpool service left the track at 70 mph and plunged down an embankment. The carriages came to a rest in a field at Ulleskelf near Tadcaster leaving twenty-two people in need of hospital treatment. A fifty-five-year-old man from Leeds was seriously hurt in the accident.

Ulleskelf Derailment
Another view of the carriages that were derailed and came to a rest in a field at Ulleskelf on 8 December 1981.

Barlby

An Intercity 125 HST passes the scene of a fatal accident on a crossing over the east coast main line in the village of Barlby, just north of Selby. Macauley William Haddock, thirteen, was in an adjacent field riding a motorcycle and crashed through the crossing gate onto the track. The east coast main line no longer passes through Barlby as it has now been diverted to the west.

Darton Derailment

Shortly after leaving North Gawber Colliery, Barnsley, six coal wagons were derailed at Darton on their way to Drax power station. The derailment, on 2 September 1983, blocked the Sheffield to Leeds route and as a result BR had to run a bus service between Darton and Wakefield Kirkgate station.

Hull Paragon Station Collision
Two passenger trains collided at Hull Paragon station on 28 January 1985, leaving passengers having to complete their journey by foot. The driver and guard needed hospital treatment as well as a female passenger who had injured her ear.

Lockington Crossing Protest
Protesters converse with a
representative from British Rail
during a protest at Lockington level
crossing on 22 August 1986.

Hutton Cranswick Crossing Protest
Hutton Cranswick, on the Hull to Scarborough line, was the site of another level crossing
protest on 2 November 1986. Here the dispute between local residents and BR had arisen
over plans to remove the full barriers and replace them with half barriers. The demonstration
drew support from other groups that objected to the plans, which were being put forward
for crossings along the Hull–Scarborough line. A contingent also came from South Woodham
Ferrers, Essex, to join the protest as their level crossing was facing the changes.

Leeds City Station Collision

Leeds Junction, 250 yards from Leeds City station, was the location of this collision, which occurred on 25 February 1988. The 7.15 a.m. Yorkshire Pullman, on the right, and the 7.15 local service to Skipton, on the left, came together resulting in the derailment of two carriages, prompting an investigation into how the two trains could converge on the same piece of track. None of the 330 passengers on the trains were injured.

Neville Hill Derailment

The derailment of this Intercity 125 carriage close to Neville Hill Carriage Depot caused chaos for commuters on17 August 1989. The accident happened at 23.30 p.m. the previous evening and had not been cleared in time for the morning rush hour, leaving many commuter services delayed or cancelled.

Pudsey Crossing Crash
Ducketts Crossing, near Pudsey, Leeds, was the scene of a fatal collision between a car and a commuter train on 4 October 1989.

Pudsey Crossing Crash
Ducketts Crossing was unmanned and required motorists to follow a set of procedures before crossing the Leeds–Bradford line. However, it was suspected that the crossing gate had been left open by a motorist who had passed through before the crash. This BR Class 155 Super Sprinter was on the line with the 16.24 p.m. service from Halifax to York when it collided with a car, dragging it 200 yards down the track. One man in the car died and another was seriously injured. None of the 100 passengers on board the train were hurt. Local residents complained the crossing was badly maintained and provided an inadequate warning that a train was approaching.

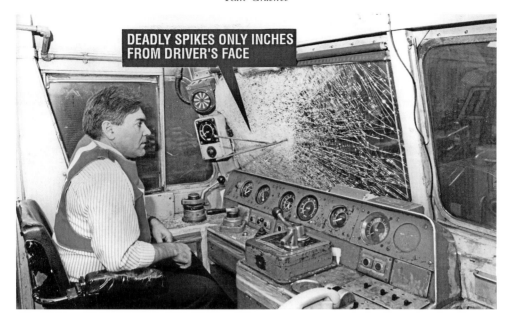

DEADLY SPIKES ONLY INCHES FROM DRIVER'S FACE

Class 47 331 Deadly Spikes
On Saturday 1 February 1992 at 8.40 p.m. the driver of a freight train headed by Class 47 locomotive no. 47 331 came within inches of being impaled on steel spikes when a lump of reinforced concrete smashed into his cab window as he passed through Fitzwilliam railway station, near Pontefract, at speed. The steel rods embedded in the concrete pierced the window after being hurled by vandals. They missed driver John Webster by inches when he ducked instinctively. He was badly shaken but otherwise unhurt. The incident happened when the train was travelling at 66 mph.

Hunslet Derailment
This diesel tanker was thrown off the track at Hunslet oil terminal after vandals wedged a stone between a set of points. BR offered a £100 reward for the culprits to be brought to justice. The photograph dates from 20 March 1992.

Holbeck Junction Collision
The front end of this Class 91 electric locomotive was left badly damaged after it collided with a 'Sprinter' DMU at Holbeck Junction, near Leeds City station, on 22 May 1992. Twenty-five people were injured in the mishap, which BR later blamed on human error.

Starbeck Crossing
Operation Zebra came to Harrogate during June 1994 and it is seen here in action at the level crossing at Starbeck. British Transport Police were behind the national campaign that was targeting drivers running red lights and dodging lowering barriers at level crossings. Officers were using a video camera to record the offenders and surface sensors to detect the speed of traffic. Starbeck crossing was one of several in Yorkshire that had been flagged as particularly troublesome. Inspector Fraser Sampson told the *Yorkshire Evening Post* that approximately six drivers had been caught during the day-long stakeout and 'we will be recommending prosecution for any drivers caught.'

CHAPTER 5
Railway Heritage Centres

York Railway Museum Reopening
During mid-July 1947 the LNER's railway museum at York was reopened by Sir Ronald Matthews (second from the left in the front row) after its closure during the war years. The LNER had opened the museum in 1928 using buildings that had formerly been fitting and machine shops in the old York & North Midland Railway Works. The collection boasted many items from the NER and GNR, but also included a number from other railway companies, such as the Great Western Railway and London & North Western Railway. The official closure came on 31 December 1973 and the buildings had been demolished by 1980.

Hudswell Clarke & Co. Ltd, Jack Lane Works, Leeds
After undergoing a major overhaul in early 1960, which included receiving a new diesel motor, *Neptune* poses in the yard of Hudswell Clarke & Co. Ltd's Jack Lane Works. The locomotive was one of two one-third scale models of Pacific engines and had been built by the Leeds company in 1931 and 1932 (*Triton*) for work on the North Bay Railway in Peasholm Park, Scarborough. In the cab of *Neptune* is Mr Leonard Tennant, a mechanical and electrical engineer from the town. Both locomotives are still at work on the NBR and have since been joined by another Pacific engine and a tank locomotive, which were also built by Hudswell Clarke & Co. Ltd.

Middleton Railway
The Middleton Railway Trust had just acquired this Leeds-built diesel locomotive reported the *Yorkshire Post* of 13 December 1967. John Fowler & Co. built the machine in 1945 and its last place of employment was George Cohen Sons & Co. Ltd, Stanningley. It is seen being shunted along a line at the trust's Hunslet headquarters by former LNER Class Y1/2 Sentinel 0-4-0T locomotive no. 54. This engine had been built in December 1933 and was originally numbered 59. Both locomotives are currently still based at the Middleton Railway.

North Yorkshire Moors Railway
Approaching Goathland station, on the Grosmont to Pickering line, is Andrew Barclay 0-6-0ST locomotive *Salmon*. The picture dates from March 1970 when the North Yorkshire Moors Railway Preservation Society was preparing for an Easter steam gala and using the line with the permission of BR. By the following year the society had become the North Yorkshire Moors Historical Railway Trust Ltd, with charitable status, allowing the line to be bought and operated for the public. The line's 18 miles were officially opened on 1 May 1973. *Salmon* has since left Yorkshire and found a new home on the Swindon and Crickdale Railway.

York Station
Passing through York station on 6 November 1974 are GNR Ivatt Large Atlantic no. 251, GNR Ivatt Small Atlantic no. 990 *Henry Oakley*, and NER Worsdell M1 Class 4-4-0 no. 1621. The locomotives were being moved from the old York Railway Museum to the new National Railway Museum. No. 251 was built at Doncaster Works in December 1902 and left service in July 1947 to be restored, almost fully, to its original GNR specifications and appearance. The engine was then stored in the Paint Shop at Doncaster and, apart from running a number of special services, did not arrive in York until 1957. No. 990 *Henry Oakley* was constructed at Doncaster in May 1898 and was withdrawn in October 1937, but it was not restored to its original design. The engine entered York Museum the following month.

York, NER No. 1621
A cosmetic overhaul is given to NER Worsdell M1 Class 4-4-0 no. 1621 during April 1975. The initial intention was for the pioneer class member, no. 1620, to be preserved, but it was withdrawn in February 1934 and later scrapped. No. 1621 was singled out for the honour when it was withdrawn in July 1945, but it did not revert back to its original condition. The chimney is positioned further forward on the smokebox to accommodate the superheater, which was an addition to the locomotive in April 1914 and the outside steam chests were removed in August 1905 to be replaced by piston valves.

York GER No. 490
The GER Class T26 2-4-0 locomotives were designed by James Holden for mixed traffic use and a total of 100 were built between 1891 and 1902 at Stratford Works; this example, GER no. 490, entered traffic in January 1895. The first class withdrawals occurred in 1926 (by now reclassified E4 by the LNER) and continued until 1940, leaving eighteen to be taken into BR stock at Nationalisation. As BR no. 62785, this locomotive was the last of the class to leave service in December 1959 and was restored to its original GER specifications at Stratford. Initially the locomotive was based at the Museum of British Transport, Clapham, but it later found a new home at York and is pictured here after arriving on 4 April 1975.

Leeds Science and Industrial Museum

There were three locomotive arrivals at the new Leeds Science and Industrial Museum at Armley Mills during March 1980. Illustrated here is a rare Thomas Green & Son Ltd 0-6-2ST locomotive, *Barber*, which was built by the company in 1908 for the 2-foot-gauge railway at Harrogate's Bilton Road gasworks. The other two locomotives to arrive were Hunslet 0-4-0WT *Jack* and Hudswell Clarke 0-4-0ST *Lord Granby*. A partial restoration of *Barber* was undertaken before the work ground to a halt in the early 1990s. By the mid-2000s an agreement was reached between Leeds City Museums and the South Tynedale Railway Preservation Society for the loan and restoration of *Barber*, and this is currently underway.

Wheldale Colliery

Hunslet-built 0-6-0ST *Wheldale* was in steam for the first time in ten years reported the *Yorkshire Evening Post* of 2 February 1982. The engine had been taken out of storage at Wheldale Colliery for fuel testing trials, but it was heading back into the pit's shed because these had been completed. Pit Mechanical Engineer Mr John Clark told the paper that he thought the engine would eventually find a new home with a preservation society – which it did with the Embsay Steam Railway.

Middleton Railway
Natalie Booth, six, is given a fireman's lift during a transport rally at the Middleton Railway on 3 July 1983 by trainee fireman Paul Whiteley. The event was hoping to prove that the railway, which was the world's oldest – having been built in 1758 – was a viable tourist attraction. Plans were underway at the time to construct a new station at Tunstall Road, which was the terminus for the 1½-mile line that ran into Middleton Park, Leeds, as well as a new shed for storing the collection of locomotives.

York
On 15 March 1983 0-6-0ST locomotive no. 1572 *Woolmer* was winched on to this low loader at York. The engine had been constructed by the Avonside Engine Co. Ltd in 1910 for work on the Longmoor Military Railway where it stayed until 1954. *Woolmer* was the first locomotive to be restored at Locomotion's Shildon Workshop in 2007 and has since been taken on loan by the Milestones Living History Museum, Basingstoke.

John Fowler & Co. Locomotive
A civic reception was held at Leeds Civic Hall on 28 March 1985 for the return of this John
Fowler & Co. 0-6-0 well tank locomotive. *Cheetal* had been working 5,000 miles away in India
since it had been constructed in Leeds in 1923. Upon its arrival the locomotive was welcomed
by a number of John Fowler & Co.'s former employees including Mr Ted Handley, pictured,
who worked for the company between 1915 and 1967 as a turner. He commented, 'I must have
worked on this engine when it was built.'

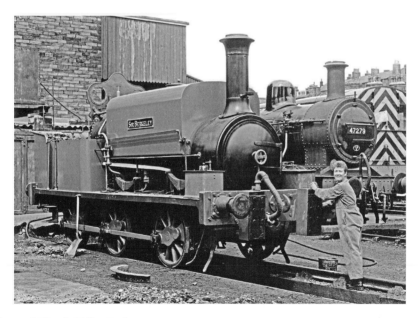

Keighley and Worth Valley Railway
Sir Berkeley receives some attention on the Keighley and Worth Valley Railway. This 0-6-0ST
locomotive was constructed by Leeds-based Manning Wardle & Co. in 1891 and during its
working life was put to work in the construction and quarrying industries. The engine was
withdrawn in 1963 and was purchased for preservation the following year, then finding a
home on the Keighley & Worth Valley Railway. Subsequently, *Sir Berkeley* was transferred
between other preserved railways and in the mid-2000s was restored again. It is currently
based on the Middleton Railway.

North Yorkshire Moors Railway, Pickering 80135
Jos de Crau is pictured at the North Yorkshire Moors Railway, Pickering, in April 1985, standing in front of the BR class four tank he owned, admiring a poster of the locomotive. 'I have great fun driving it occasionally, under supervision,' explained Jos, who was managing director of a group of companies in Holland. He lived near The Hague and was introduced to the North Yorkshire Moors Railway by a friend at Harrogate with whom he corresponded to improve his English.

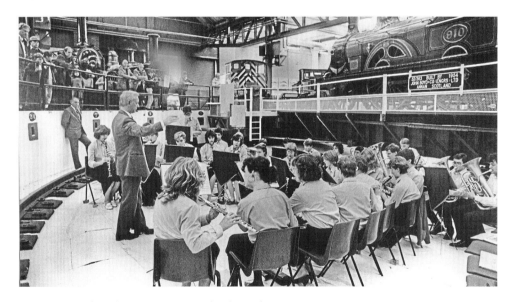

York, National Railway Museum – School Band
The bottom of a turntable pit is the last place anyone would expect to find an orchestra. But on the 25 October 1986 the senior concert band from the York Music Centre performed for over an hour at the National Railway Museum as part of the former's programme of public performances. The band, with members aged between thirteen and eighteen, were led by Mr Kenneth Jackson, who told the *Yorkshire Post* that the concert had been well received by visitors to the NRM. On the turntable to the right is NER Fletcher 2-4-0 no. 910, which was in service between 1875 and 1925.

North Yorkshire Moors Railway, Preserved Deltic

Murray Brown, Chairman of the Deltic Preservation Society, poses with one of the group's locomotives during April 1988. The society was formed in 1977 after it became clear that the class was going to be withdrawn and scrapped due to the introduction of the Class 43 High Speed Train. By the early 1980s the DPS had raised enough funds to purchase two BR Class 55 locomotives, D9009 (55 009) *Alycidon* and D9019 (55 019) *Royal Highland Fusilier*, which had been withdrawn in January 1982 and December 1981 respectively. In the mid-1980s a third Class 55, D9015 (55 015) *Tulyar*, which had been bought privately from BR, was sold to the group.

Castleford, St Aidan's Open Cast Mine

Peter Rhodes, top foreman at St Aidan's open cast coalmine near Castleford, bids a fond farewell to this former BR Class 03 0-6-0 diesel-mechanical shunter in March 1987. The locomotive had been working at the mine for fourteen years and was to find a new home on the preserved railway at Steamport in Southport. Swindon Works had erected the shunter, BR no. D2148, in May 1960 and it spent its career in BR's North Eastern region before being withdrawn in November 1972. Steamport has since become the Ribble Steam Railway and Museum after a change of locations, but they are still in possession of the locomotive, which has unfortunately seen only sporadic operation due to mechanical issues.

EM2 27000

This BR EM2 (later Class 77) electric locomotive no. 27000 (later E27000) *Electra* was built at Gorton Works in December 1953 and was in service until October 1968. All seven of the EM2 locomotives were later sold to Nederlandse Spoorwegen, becoming their 1500 Class; no. 27000 worked for them as no. 1502 until June 1986. The EM2 Locomotive Society then purchased *Electra* from NS and was repatriated to be housed at the Midland Railway, Butterley. During mid-1988 the locomotive was moved to Bradford, under the auspices of the West Yorkshire Transport Museum, who had the necessary facilities for a cosmetic restoration of *Electra*. The EM2 Locomotive Society's publicity officer Mr Charles Petty (leaning from the cab) and WYTM project development officer Mr John Moor (on the footsteps) are pictured with the locomotive on 16 January 1989.

Embsay Steam Railway

Colleagues reunite for work at the Embsay Steam Railway during April 1989. Colin Davis, pictured, drove NCB no. S134 *Wheldale* during his career as a driver for the NCB and had also been involved in its restoration for hauling passengers on the line. The locomotive had been built by Hunslet in 1944 for the War Department and after leaving the forces the NCB employed the engine at Wheldale Colliery until they retired it in 1982. *Wheldale* was operational at Embsay until the need for repairs curtailed its new career. The locomotive is currently at the railway awaiting restoration.

North Yorkshire Moors Railway
Jos de Crau from Amsterdam poses in front of his two locomotives at work on the North Yorkshire Moors Railway during 1990. BR Standard Class 4MT 2-6-4T no. 80135, built in April 1956, was rescued from Barry scrap yard and arrived at Pickering in March 1973. The locomotive was subsequently acquired by Jos who financed its restoration in the NYMR's workshops. He also owned BR Sulzer Type 2 (Class 25/3) 'Bo-Bo' locomotive D7628 (later TOPS 25 278 and named *Sybilla*, after his mother). The locomotive was built by Beyer Peacock in Manchester in August 1965 and withdrawn in March 1987.

Embsay Steam Railway
Fireman Harry Ferris throws another shovel of coal into the firebox of this Hunslet 0-6-0ST no. S121 *Primrose No. 2.* The locomotive was constructed in 1952 and worked for the NCB before being preserved on the Embsay Steam Railway. However, it was withdrawn in 1999 for major repairs and is yet to re-enter traffic. The Embsay Steam Railway is now known as the Embsay & Bolton Abbey Steam Railway. Bolton Abbey station was re-opened and added to the line in 1998. The photograph dates from 6 October 1990.

Kirklees Light Railway
Fox, a 2-6-2T locomotive based on a Hunslet engine, stops at Cuckoo's Nest station on the opening day of Kirklees Light Railway in late 1991. The 15-in.-gauge railway occupies part of the former trackbed of the Lancashire & Yorkshire Railway's branch line between Shepley Junction, on the Penistone line, and Clayton West. Watching the arrival is platelayer Mr Mel Eva, while Mr Brian Taylor drives the locomotive.

CHAPTER 6
Staff

Sheffield, Women Platelayers
These women from Sheffield were playing their part during the Second World War by turning their hand to platelaying on lines in the Sheffield district. The women, aged between twenty-three and thirty-six, were the only ones to be taking up such a task in the north of England. The picture dates from July 1942.

Track Inspectors
Mr A. Pownder moistens the track for Mr D. Butler to test for faults in the metal with an electronic tester. Mr H. Pratt, in the background, watches for trains approaching the men. The picture dates from 17 November 1967.

Healey Mills Marshalling Yard
Opened by the North Eastern Region in the early 1960s on a 140-acre site, Healey Mills Marshalling Yard was the largest in Yorkshire. It was hoped that the yard would streamline the flow of freight and mineral traffic through the county. Plenty of experience was at hand for BR to achieve this aim in the form of these three men, pictured on 25 November 1964, who worked as cutters in the reception sidings. They had 130 years experience in the railway industry between them. From left to right, they are Clifford Collier (forty-eight years), Sid Newsome (forty-two years) and Fred Horne (forty years).

Knottingley Level Crossing Workmen

Men working on the line at England Lane level crossing, Knottingley, were praised after they completed their work efficiently and on time, allaying the fears of locals that it would cause much disruption. Delays of two minutes were averted after a diversion, taking traffic through a yard, was put in place. A BR official announced, 'It went like clockwork.' The Goole to Wakefield line, which required the work, had sunk below normal levels and the men were banking up the track.

Ripon

The Leeds & Thirsk Railway (Leeds Northern Railway from 1851) opened their first section of line between Thirsk and Ripon to the general public on 1 June 1848. The track between Weeton and Wormald Green was completed on 1 September and the latter was connected to Ripon by mid-September, crossing the River Ure to the south end of the station. The lines to Ripon from Harrogate, Northallerton and Thirsk operated for almost 120 years, but they were closed on 6 March 1967. In this picture the track is prised from its chairs by workers on the cast-iron railway bridge over the River Ure at Ripon on 16 September 1970 as part of the removal of the line.

York, NRM

New British Railways uniforms were unveiled on 20 February 1979 amongst the historic locomotives at the NRM. The garments were dark blue, made from a synthetic material and featured coloured collars that indicated the rank of the employee to the public and enthusiasts; caps also had a coloured band for this purpose. Red was used for railmen and leading railmen, while blue was used for senior railmen and chargemen. Modelling the uniform (from left to right) are Mr Harry Apedaile, reservations porter, Mr Brian Scaife, leading railman, and Mr John Bruckwicki, senior railman.

Mirfield Station

Thomas the cat was a firm favourite with passengers using Mirfield station, and when he became ill in the latter months of 1975 (losing an eye in a fight with another feline) he was inundated with tasty treats to help him on the road to recovery. To express his thanks, as well as a happy Christmas to commuters, Thomas organised this notice to placed in the booking office of Mirfield station and he is helped by porter Raymond Willingham.

CHAPTER 7
Bridges, New Routes, Signal Boxes and Tunnels

Whitby Ticket Office
This structure was the original ticket office for the Whitby & Pickering Railway and it was located close to the present station. The Act for the railway was passed in May 1833 with George Stephenson being employed as the line's engineer. The official opening came three years later on 26 May 1836 with six carriages, each drawn by a horse, taking passengers along the line. In mid-1845 the W&PR was taken over by the York & North Midland Railway and the company began to rebuild the line for use by steam locomotives; this was completed in July 1847.

Huddersfield Lockwood Viaduct

Lockwood viaduct was constructed during the mid- to late 1840s on the Huddersfield & Sheffield Junction Railway line, which ran between Huddersfield and the Manchester, Sheffield and Lincolnshire line, joining it near Penistone. The viaduct spans the valley of the River Holme and it has thirty-four arches, is approximately 476 yards long, and approximately 130 ft high and 30 ft wide at the top. These men are not admiring this feat of engineering as may be expected, or even debating the design chosen by John Hawkshaw. They are trying to answer a question asked by many a Huddersfield resident: can a cricket ball be thrown over the viaduct? *The Yorkshire Evening Post* of 16 September 1938 reported that Jack Crumms of Armitage Bridge, Huddersfield, had proved that it could!

Brotherton Tunnel

A 3-mile-long (approx.) branch line from the York & North Midland Railway line at Burton Salmon to Knottingley, on the Wakefield, Pontefract & Goole Railway line, was built in the late 1840s by the former company in a strategic move, orchestrated by George Hudson, to stop the GNR building its own line to York. The line featured a tunnel at Brotherton, which was originally meant to be 100 yards long, but because of an objection to this from Sir John William Ramsden of Byram Hall, the tunnel was extended a further 219 yards. The reason for this was that the line passed the Byram Hall and he did not want to see the smoke and steam from the locomotives. During 1952 a section of the tunnel, 215 yards long, was removed to reduce maintenance costs.

Skipton Station
This Pullman coach was sold to the Midland Railway by the American company in the latter half of the nineteenth century for services between London St Pancras and Scotland via Manchester. When the coaches were withdrawn from service, instead of being scrapped (they were seen as too good to be broken up), a new role was found for them as stationary stores and canteens placed around the MR network. This example found a home at the end of platform 2 at Skipton station.

Bradford Forster Square Station
The forerunner of Bradford's Forster Square station was opened by the Leeds & Bradford Railway on 1 July 1846 and was known as Bradford Market Street station. The L&BR was subsequently absorbed into the Midland Railway during the early 1850s and by the final decade of the nineteenth century, the MR had erected a new station, which acquired the Forster Square name, in June 1924. The entrance to the station is pictured here on 19 October 1962, from Forster Square. On 11 June 1990, the station reopened after it had been moved to the north and the land was later reused for offices; a Royal Mail sorting office also occupies part of the site. Forster Square has been enveloped by a stalled shopping centre development.

Ben Rhydding Station
A first generation DMU passes through Ben Rhydding station during September 1963. The station was opened on 1 August 1865 by the Ben Rhydding Hydro as a private stop on the newly constructed Otley & Ilkley Joint Railway. The MR then bought the stop and it was opened to the public on 1 July 1866. The facilities were of a temporary nature and it was not until 1871 that the permanent station, consisting of the buildings seen here, was erected at the expense of the Ben Rhydding Hydro. The village that the railway runs through was originally named Wheatley, but it too fell under the influence of the Hydro and the change of name occurred in the early twentieth century. The station buildings have since been demolished and replaced with metal-framed plastic-covered shelters.

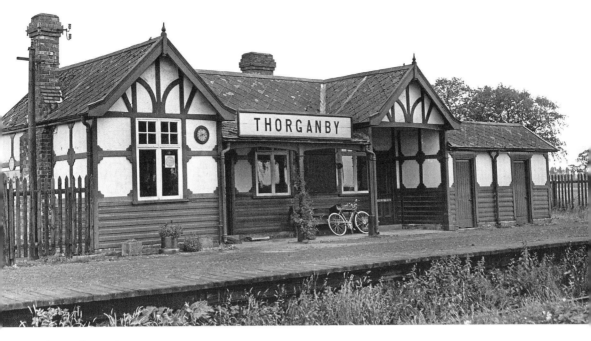

Thorganby Station

Escrick and Riccall Rural District Councils were granted an Order by the Light Railway Commission on 29 September 1899 to construct a line from Foss Islands, York, to Cliff Common, near Selby. The main purpose of the Derwent Valley Light Railway line was to transport minerals and goods, then passengers, to the major population centres in the area. Financial problems, however, meant that construction of the line was not completed until 1913. The ceremonial first trip took place on 19 July, before opening to the public on 21 July 1913. Passenger numbers during the First World War were quite high, being in the high-40,000s, but by the mid-1920s this had dwindled to 18,427 per year and regular passenger services were withdrawn on 1 September 1926. Thorganby station is pictured during July 1964 when part of the southern section was to close. Service on the line was stopped fully on 27 September 1981.

Healey Mills Marshalling Yard Signal Box

A scene in Healey Mills signal box, which was captured on 25 November 1964. Signalman Walter Sinkinson and Relief Signalman Frank Senior watch the map of the yard, which lit up when a line was occupied.

Gildersome Tunnel
Mr Percy Richardson (left) and Mr Bill Dix (right) pause for a detailed inspection of the track in Gildersome tunnel, which had been condemned. The tunnel was situated on the LNWR's Heaton Lodge–Farnley Junction line (Leeds New Line and originally called the Heaton Lodge & Wortley Railway). The tunnel stretched for one mile and 571 yards. The Leeds New Line, opened in October 1900, was later known as the Spen Valley Line. Closure to passengers occurred in August 1965. The *Yorkshire Evening Post* of 25 March 1965 stated: 'For 65 years the Gildersome tunnel ... has carried trains through the shoulder of upland between Morley and Gildersome. But soon the echoes of the last train will die away'. The picture dates from 23 March 1965.

Hampsthwaite Station
The NER began construction of the Nidd Valley Railway in the early 1860s and opened the line, which ran from the Leeds–Northallerton route near Killinghall to Pateley Bridge, on 1 May 1862. Three stations originally existed on the line and a further two were later added, with Hampsthwaite station being the final addition. Although a specific opening date has become obscure, Quick (2009) notes that its first appearance in *Bradshaw's Timetable* was September 1866. The line was mainly used by mineral traffic and a goods service was operated until the mid-1960s, however, passenger services were not well-used and were withdrawn at the start of the 1950s. Hampsthwaite station closed on 2 January 1950. Miss Margaret Cooper-Ross is pictured at the station in September 1965 when there were plans to turn the old trackbed into a public footpath. The station house still stands as a private residence.

Dacre Station
Also pictured in September 1965 is Dacre station, which was another station on the Nidd Valley line, situated between Pateley Bridge and Darley. It was opened on 1 May 1862 with the name Dacre Banks, which lasted until 1866. Dacre station closed on 2 April 1951, and like Hampsthwaite station house, it has survived as a private residence.

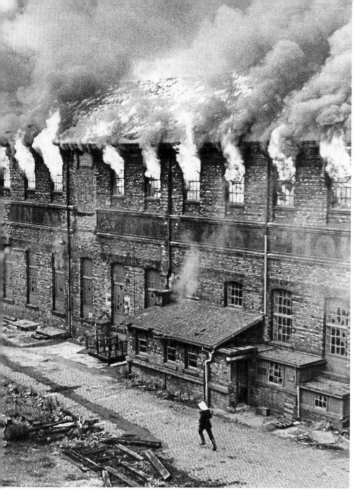

Wicker Goods Depot Fire
Sheffield was unceremoniously brushed aside when George Stephenson was planning the North Midland Railway line between Derby and Leeds because of steep gradients that the line would encounter around the city. The Sheffield and Rotherham Railway set about planning a route to join the NMR line at Rotherham, which was connected in May 1840, but the line had already opened to traffic on 1 November 1838 between Sheffield (Wicker from 1852/1853) station and Rotherham (Westgate from 1896) station. The MR opened a new station in Sheffield on 1 February 1870 leaving Sheffield Wicker to become the company's goods station. The building was upgraded in the 1890s and was in use until July 1965. On the 31 July 1966 the station was gutted by fire, the aftermath of which is seen here. The land was subsequently cleared and for a time accommodated car dealerships before a supermarket was recently erected on the site.

Bardsey Station

Bardsey station was located on the branch line between Cross Gates, Leeds and Wetherby, which was opened by the NER on 1 May 1876. The 10½ miles covered by the line initially only had a single track, but this was doubled in 1902. The line closed to passengers on 6 January 1964 and to goods on 27 April. Bardsey station house has been pictured during 1968 when it had fallen into a state of neglect. Plans were afoot to demolish the station and build a housing estate on the land, which eventually occurred.

Ingleton Station

The first station at Ingleton was opened by the ('Little') North Western Railway on 31 July 1849 with the section of the company's line from Skipton. However, the station was closed on 1 June 1850 as the intended line from Ingleton to the Lancashire & Carlisle Railway near Tebay was abandoned due to the cost and difficulty of constructing it. A route branching to Lancaster in the west was laid instead, leaving the original line at Clapham Junction, forcing the closure of Ingleton. The L&CR resurrected and amended the NWR's planned line between Ingleton and Tebay and built the route between 1858 and 1861. The NWR line and station (now under the ownership of the MR) was then reopened on 1 October 1861, but the station was subsequently rebuilt by the company. It outlasted the station of the same name built by the London & North Western Railway (successor of the L&CR) by thirty-seven years and closed on 1 February 1954. The station is pictured, in a derelict state, on 16 August 1970 and it has since been demolished.

Left: **Standege Tunnel**
During October 1970, Standege tunnel – eighty years old and on the Huddersfield–Manchester line – was modernised by BR. The work was scheduled to take six months, with the involvement of thirty men working Saturday nights and Sunday. Pictured here is one of the excavators that were being used to remove a thick layer of old shale ballast from the tunnel floor as the build up had caused the space inside to be reduced.

Below: **Standege Tunnel**
A view inside Standege tunnel. The wagons on the right hold new ballast, which once deposited, would have 60-foot lengths of track laid on top.

Sheffield Midland Station Signal Box
The Lord Mayor of Sheffield Ald. S. Kenneth Arnold (centre) is pictured in the relay room at Sheffield Midland station's new power signal box during 1973. Mr W. G. Boddy (right), the divisional signal and telecommunications engineer, explains the system to the gathering. Mr J. B. Peile, a member of BR's Eastern Region board, is standing against the pillar.

Sheffield Midland Station Signal Box
Ald. S Kenneth Arnold continues the tour of Sheffield Midland station's power signal box. He is seen here with the control panel, which was explained by Signalman Mr Bernard Knipe (left), and standing behind the men is Mr Harry Amos, divisional operating manager. The power signal box became operational in late January 1973 at a cost of £2 million. It replaced Heeley station, Heeley sidings, Millhouses, Sheffield A, B, No. 1, No. 2, and Queen's Road.

Selby Diversion

This aerial view shows the east coast main line (to the right) and the Selby diversion (to the left) at Temple Hirst. The change of route occurred to allow a valuable seam of coal present under east coast main line to be extracted, and the diversion was funded by the NCB at an estimated cost of £30 million. There were also concerns that mining subsidence would have a negative impact on the track and any defects would be amplified by the introduction of new high speeds trains. Approximately 14 miles of new track was laid and it rejoined the old route at Colton, 5 miles to the south of York.

Selby Diversion
A. Monk & Co. Ltd was given the contract for the construction of the Selby diversion and work commenced on 4 April 1980; a ceremonial foundation stone was laid on 30 July. Progress at Hambleton is seen from the air on 27 January 1981 where the east coast main line and the Leeds to Selby line (running from right to left) intersect at Hambleton Junction. The beginnings of the bridge that takes the Leeds–Selby line over the east coast main line can be seen in the centre of the picture.

Tinsley East Junction Signal Box
A derelict Tinsley East Junction signal box has been photographed during mid-1985. It is possible that a coal train is passing on its way to Tinsley Marshalling Yard, headed by a pair of Class 20s. The signal box was on the Manchester, Sheffield and Lincolnshire Railway extension from Tinsley to Rotherham, which left the South Yorkshire Railway's Blackburn Valley line (taken over by the MS&L in the early 1860s), and opened in the early 1870s.

Left: **Summit Tunnel**
Summit tunnel, on the Greater Manchester–West Yorkshire border, was ready to reopen in August 1985 after being closed for nearly eight months. This was because of a serious fire on 20 December 1984, which involved a train of thirteen petrol tanks that had partially derailed inside the tunnel. Fire crews fought the blaze until 24 December and were present at the scene for some time afterwards. Minimal damage was caused to the tunnel, but the track and signalling equipment had to be renewed. Todmorden station was chosen for the official reopening of Summit tunnel and the ceremony was to be carried out by the general manager of BR's London Midland Region on Monday, 19 August 1985.

Below: **Harrogate**
Engineers are pictured at work installing safety barriers on the Skipton Road bridge, Harrogate. The angled metal coping was an attempt to foil would-be daredevils from climbing on the edges of the bridge and falling onto the track below. The bridge, over the York to Harrogate line, acquired the feature during May 1988.

Burley Park Station
A BR Class 144 'Pacer' DMU has stopped at Burley Park station, Leeds, on 28 November 1988 – the day of the station's opening. It is the first stop on the line to Harrogate and then York, which makes it suitable for commuters to these places. Northern Rail currently operates the station, which offers little in the way of facilities.

Sculcoates Goods Station, Hull
Railway enthusiast Mr John Morfin poses outside the former Sculcoates Goods station, Wincolmlee, Hull, on 10 February 1989 after the building had been given Grade II listed status. Mr Morfin had encouraged the Environment Department to list the structure, which had been constructed in 1864 for the NER to the design of Thomas Prosser, as it was the oldest large town or city goods station of the NER's left standing. The building ceased to be used for railway purposes in 1965 and was later bought by the Humberside County Council. Deputy leader of the Council, Councillor Tony Fee, told the *Yorkshire Post* that the listing decision had been a surprise and was concerned that future users of the building would be put off by its status.

Ilkley Station

Ilkley station was opened on 1 August 1865 as the terminus for the Otley & Ilkley Joint Railway. The MR took charge of construction of the station and employed their architect John Holloway Sanders to produce the design. It was Italianate in style with an entrance inspired by a Venetian window (seen here). The entrance led into a large booking hall, which had waiting rooms placed at either side. When the line was extended to Skipton in 1888, the platform area was extended and received a roof and other MR station features. In the late 1980s the station building was taken out of railway use and transformed into a supermarket and retail area.

Bridge for Leeds–Selby Line

Engineers were in a race against time during the weekend of 25/26 April 1992 as they only had fifty-seven hours to install a 2,200-ton bridge for the Leeds to Selby railway line. They also had to remove 10,000 tons of railway embankment, as well as the old track and signalling before the bridge could be put in position. The line had to be moved to allow the construction of the South Milford/Sherburn-in-Elmet bypass, which is also seen in the midst of construction.

Right & below: **Woodburn Junction Signal Box**

Woodburn Junction was located on the first section of the Sheffield & Lincolnshire Junction Railway line, which opened between Sheffield Bridgehouses station and Beighton on 12 February 1849; the line was completed to Gainsborough on 17 July. By this time S&LJR had merged with the Sheffield, Ashton-under-Lyne & Manchester Railway and Great Grimsby & Sheffield Junction Railway to form the Manchester, Sheffield & Lincolnshire Railway, which linked Manchester with the port at Grimsby. On 1 August 1864 the South Yorkshire Railway opened their extension from the Blackburn Valley line at Meadowhall to the MS&L line, thus forming Woodburn Junction. It was also utilised from 11 May 1895 by the London & North Western Railway for spur to their Sheffield City goods station, later Sheffield Nunnery goods station.

Left: **Kirkstall Signal Box**
Signalman Brian Marshall is pictured in his signal box at Kirkstall Junction, Leeds, on 16 April 1993, with no trains to control that day because of a one-day strike by ASLEF. Dating from 1910, the box was originally known as Kirkstall Station Junction signal box and located by the Up Main line. It took the Kirkstall Junction name in the early 1930s. Closure came on 4 June 1994 when control of trains passed to Leeds power signal box. Shortly afterwards the structure was demolished.

Below: **Guiseley Station**
Guiseley station was also on the Otley & Ilkley Joint Railway and opened on 1 August 1865 with this footbridge providing access to both sides of the station. During the early 1990s a scheme to electrify the route begun and it was necessary to remove the bridge, which brought vociferous condemnation from local resident Mr Colin Whitaker. The bridge was to find a new home over the Settle to Carlisle railway line.

Bibliography

Anderson, Robert and Peter Rose, *Railway Memories No. 22: Return to Leeds*, 2009

Bairstow, Martin, *The Keighley and Worth Valley Railway: A Guide and History*, 1991

Bairstow, Martin, *Railways Around Whitby Volume One*, 1998

Binns, Donald, *The 'Little' North Western Railway: Skipton-Ingleton, Clapham-Lancaster & Morecambe*, 1982

Buck, Martin and Mark Rawlinson, *Line by Line: The East Coast Main Line Kings Cross to Edinburgh*, 2002

Buck, Martin and Mark Rawlinson, *Line by Line: The Midland Route London St. Pancras to Glasgow Central*, 2004

Clay, John F., *The Stanier Black Fives*, 1974

Clough, David N., *British Rail Standard Diesels of the 1960s*, 2009

Dow, George, *Great Central Volume One: The Progenitors 1813-1863*, 1985

Fawcett, Bill, *A History of North Eastern Railway Architecture Volume Two: A Mature Art*, 2003

Griffiths, Roger and John Hooper, *Great Northern Railway Engine Sheds Volume 3: Yorkshire and Lancashire*, 2000

Griffiths, Roger and Paul Smith, *The Directory of British Engine Sheds and Principal Locomotive Servicing Points: 2*, 2000,

Grindlay, Jim, *British Railways Steam Locomotive Allocations 1948-1968: Part Three London Midland and Scottish Regions 40001-58937*, 2008

Groves, N., *Great Northern Locomotive History Volume 3A: 1896-1911 The Ivatt Era*, 1990

Guppy, Antony, *BR Class 55 Diesels: The Deltics*, 1981

Haigh, Alan J., *Railways and Tramways in the City of Leeds*, 2010

Hallas, Christine, *The Wensleydale Railway*, 2002

Haresnape, Brian, *Fowler Locomotives: A Pictorial History*, 1997

Haresnape, Brian, *Stanier Locomotives: A Pictorial History*, 1974

Hoole, Ken, *A Regional History of the Railways of Great Britain Volume 4: The North East*, 1974

Hoole, Ken, *North Eastern Locomotive Sheds*, 1972

Hoole, Ken, *Rail Centres: York*, 1983

Hunt, David, Fred James and Bob Essery with John Jennison and David Clarke, *LMS Locomotive Profiles No. 5: The Mixed Traffic Class 5s – Nos. 5000-5224*, 2003

Hunt, David, Fred James and Bob Essery with John Jennison and David Clarke, *LMS Locomotive Profiles No. 6: The Mixed Traffic Class 5s – Nos. 5225-5499 and 4658-4999*, 2004

Hunt, David, Fred James, John Jennison and Bob Essery, *LMS Locomotive Profiles No. 7: The Mixed Traffic Class 5s - Caprotti Valve Gear Engines*, 2006

Hunt, David, John Jennison, Fred James and Bob Essery, *LMS locomotive Profiles No. 8: The Class 8F 2-8-0s*, 2005

Joy, David, *A Regional History of the Railways of Great Britain Volume 8: South and West Yorkshire*, 1984

Longworth, Hugh, *British Railways First Generation DMUs*, 2011

Marsden, Colin J., *Traction Recognition*, 2008

Mason, P. G., *Lost Railways of East Yorkshire*, 1997

Parkin, Keith, *British Railways Mark One Coaches*, 2006

Quick, Michael, *Railway Passenger Stations in Great Britain: A Chronology*, 2009

RCTS, *Locomotives of the LNER: Part 1 Preliminary Survey*, 1963

RCTS, *Locomotives of the LNER: Part 2A Tender Engines – Classes A1 to A10*, 1978

RCTS, *Locomotives of the LNER: Part 2B Tender Engines – Classes B1 to B19*, 1975

RCTS, *Locomotives of the LNER: Part 3B Tender Engines – Classes D1 to 12*, 1980

RCTS, *Locomotives of the LNER: Part 3C Tender Engines – Classes D13 to D24*, 1981

RCTS, *Locomotives of the LNER: Part 4 Tender Engines – Classes D25 to E7*, 1968

RCTS, *Locomotives of the LNER: Part 6B Tender Engines – Classes O1 to P2*, 1991

RCTS, *Locomotives of the LNER: Part 6C Tender Engines – Classes Q1 to Y10*, 1984

RCTS, *Locomotives of the LNER: Part 9B Tank Engines – Classes Q1 to Z5*, 1977

RCTS, *Locomotives of the LNER: Part 10A Departmental Stock, Locomotive Sheds, Boiler and Tender Numbering*, 1991

Reading, S. J., *The Derwent Valley Light Railway*, 1967

Sixsmith, Ian, *The Book of the Ivatt 4MTs: LM Class 4 2-6-0s*, 2012

Townsin, Ray, *The Jubilee 4-6-0's*, 2006

Walmsley, Tony, *Shed by Shed Part One: London Midland*, 2010

Walmsley, Tony, *Shed by Shed Part Two: Eastern*, 2010

Yeadon, W. B., *Yeadon's Register of LNER Locomotives Volume One: Gresley A1 and A3 Classes*, 2001

Yeadon, W. B., *Yeadon's Register of LNER Locomotives Volume Two: Gresley A4 and W1 Classes*, 2001

Yeadon, W. B., *Yeadon's Register of LNER Locomotives Volume Three: Raven, Thompson & Peppercorn Pacifics*, 2001

Yeadon, W. B., *Yeadon's Register of LNER Locomotives Volume Four: Gresley V2 and V4 Classes*, 2001

Yeadon, W. B., *Yeadon's Register of LNER Locomotives Volume Six: Thompson B1 Class*, 2001

Yeadon, W. B., *Yeadon's Register of LNER Locomotives Volume Nine: Gresley 8-Coupled Engines Classes O1, O2, P1, P2 and U1*, 1995